Panic Attacks

A NATURAL APPROACH

Panic Attacks

A NATURAL APPROACH

Shirley Trickett

Ulysses Press  Berkeley, CA
1999

Published by: Ulysses Press
P.O. Box 3440
Berkeley, CA 94703-3440

Library of Congress Catalog Card Number: 99-60326

ISBN: 1-56975-187-0

First published as *Coping Successfully with Panic Attacks* by Sheldon Press

Printed in Canada by Transcontinental Printing

10 9 8 7 6 5 4

Editor: Kathy Kaiser
Cover Design: Sara Glaser, Leslie Henriques
Cover Illustration: "City Crowd" Diane Ong/SuperStock Fine Arts
Interior Illustrations: Claudine Gossett
Editorial and production staff: David Wells, Paul de Benedictis, Natasha Lay
Indexer: Sayre Van Young

Distributed in the United States by Publishers Group West and in Canada by Raincoast Books.

Contents

Note from the Publisher

This book has been written and published strictly for informational purposes, and *in no way should it be used as a substitute for consultation with your medical doctor or health care professional*. Before using self-help methods, you are advised to take your health problems to your physician. All facts in this book came from medical files, clinical journals, scientific publications, personal interviews, published trade books, self-published materials by experts, magazine articles, and the personal-practice experiences of the authorities quoted or sources cited. You should not consider educational material herein to be the practice of medicine or to replace consultation with a physician or other medical practitioner. The author and publisher are providing you with information in this work so that you can have the knowledge and can choose, at your own risk, to act on that knowledge. The author and publisher also urge all readers to be aware of their health status and to consult health professionals before beginning any health program, including changes in dietary habits.

The author and publisher welcome your comments and suggestions for future editions. We would also appreciate hearing how this book has helped you. Please contact us at Ulysses Press, P.O. Box 3440, Berkeley, CA 94703; readermail@ulyssespress.com.

Introduction

I trust you will find this an optimistic book with a common-sense approach to the very distressing problem of panic attacks. I have written it because I get so many requests for information on this subject. In it, I seek to comfort and reassure, and to stress what I firmly believe: panic attacks are curable. Yes, curable. I don't pretend that by reading the following chapters you are going to have all the answers, or that the methods I describe are going to work overnight. What I do hope is that when you fully understand what is happening to you during a panic attack, you will become less afraid and accept that panic attacks do not drop from the sky onto helpless people; there is always an underlying reason.

You Are Causing Your Panic Attacks

I run the risk of your wanting to light the barbecue with this book before reading any further. You are probably thinking *who* would possibly want to give him or herself these attacks? The full horror of a panic attack cannot be understood unless you have experienced one, so for me to suggest that you are responsible for the dreaded episodes could be irritating to say the least. I hope you will forgive this statement when I explain that I include myself in this. I rarely write about anything unless I have firsthand knowledge and I assure you that I can describe a panic attack, in every fearful detail, from my own experience.

Sharing the Experience

It is often very difficult to convince people that the symptoms they are experiencing are panic attacks. It is even harder to get them to accept that they can take control of the situation and learn to manage the attacks, or get rid of them altogether. I find working with groups of people who suffer panic attacks very rewarding and effective. I have often talked myself hoarse in a one-to-one session without a great deal of success, only to find that when sufferers attended a group and listened to the experiences of others they were instantly reassured. Some of these experiences are shared with you in this book. Several types of panic attacks are described in the hope that you will find one similar to your experience; but, remember, you are unlikely to find a mirror image of your own unique symptoms.

What This Book Has to Offer

The philosophy in this book is one of the physical management of anxiety: how to regulate your breathing; how to adjust blood sugar levels; and how to release muscle spasms in order to slow down the production of adrenaline (the overproduction of which is the main cause of panic attacks). What happens to the body when the emergency button is being pressed continuously is discussed fully in Part One, while self-help methods that will enable you to take your finger off the button are explained in Part Two. The suggestions in Part Two will not make sense unless you understand why your body behaves the way it does, so do not be tempted to turn straight to the self-help section. Part One also helps you to turn sleuth and track down where your symptoms are coming from. You may be surprised by some of the possible causes of panic attacks.

You don't have to be "high strung" to get panic attacks. Many believe panic attacks are only experienced by those who are already over-anxious. This has not been my experience. I have seen many people who have suffered panic attacks that derived from purely physical causes such as dieting, prolonged exercise, or drug reactions.

Working Through the Book

While my initial approach to curing panic attacks is through the management of body functions, emotional and spiritual health are also discussed. Wholeness comes from the harmony of body, mind, and spirit. Looking after your body paves the way to peace of mind, which in turn allows you to connect with what I believe is the most important part of you: your soul, spirit, essence, or inner being— whatever name you give it. Unconditionally loving the person you find on your inner journey is a key step toward wholeness.

This book discusses why symptoms are often dismissed or over-looked. It also gives several medical references on the subject of hyperventilation, the main cause of symptoms of panic attacks. If you are receiving medical treatment, such as medication, this book is not meant to replace it, but rather to work alongside it. What you might find, however, is that when you are educated about your body and its responses, you are able to reduce your use of tranquilizers or antidepressants, or come off them altogether.

Please note: Do not make any changes in your medication without your doctor's approval and without full instruction on withdrawal methods. It is also important *not* to use any of the dietary advice contained in this book if it conflicts with a diet provided by your doctor.

PART ONE
Knowing Yourself

CHAPTER ONE

The Dreaded Panic Attack

Men are flesh and blood and apprehensive.

—Shakespeare, *Julius Caesar*

What Is a Panic Attack?

A panic attack is an exaggeration of the body's normal response to fear. The chemical adrenaline, which is normally produced when we need action—to run from danger, to fight, or even to get angry—is overproduced, and the result is a multitude of unpleasant sensations and a distressing degree of fear. It is a pity that these physical and emotional feelings have been labeled panic attacks. The word *attack* suggests illness, something that has to be endured, an episode that the sufferer is powerless to avoid or control. You will see that this is not so. Better terms for these responses are adrenaline flushes or adrenaline surges. These terms describe exactly what is happening and sound much less alarming.

What Does It Feel Like to Be Overflowing with Adrenaline?

During an adrenaline surge, the body behaves like an old Charlie Chaplin film or a video on fast forward: everything is running at top speed. Your breathing rate increases, your heart beats faster, your blood pressure rises, and thoughts race around in your head. Every system in the body is affected, including the digestive system; so the panic attack sufferer may experience an urgent need to go to the bathroom.

What Does a Panic Attack Feel Like?

Sandra: I feel convinced that something terrible is about to happen, and I shake from head to foot. My mouth goes dry and I feel like I can't swallow. It usually happens in a shop. When I get out into the fresh air, the feeling goes away.

Mark: I feel very weak, as if I'm going to faint, and I have trouble getting a good breath. I sweat and my girlfriend says I go pale. I feel so helpless when it happens, and I'm always convinced I'm dying. I feel like such a fool afterward.

Peter: I feel suddenly overcome by terror: my heart races and I want to run. I must leave wherever I am and get home as quickly as possible. I never get these feelings at home.

Marjory: My thoughts are so weird, and my words sound odd to me. I always feel as if I'm having a stroke. Everything around me looks strange. I seem to seize up with fear each time, and it takes a lot to convince me at the time that it is just a panic attack. I'm willing to accept this later, but not at the time. In fact, I get quite irritated if anyone suggests that it is nerves.

Pablo: It's as though a sudden deep depression jumps out of nowhere. I'm anxious, too, but seem to be more aware of the gloom. I feel utterly hopeless when this happens and am often miserable for a couple of days afterward. When I have recovered and analyze it, I can usually see that anxiety starts it off, although that does not occur to me at the time. I live in dread of another attack for a few days.

Symptoms of a Panic Attack

The following list of symptoms is meant to be encouraging, not daunting. It should convince you that this simple opening of the adrenaline floodgates can cause all the funny feelings you are getting, and more:

- *Fear.* You may have a sudden fear of the world coming to an end, of dying, going mad, having a heart attack, having a stroke, losing control, fainting, being incontinent, being sick, shouting, looking foolish, running, or the unknown.

- *Bewilderment.* When they are in the middle of it, even regular sufferers can find it difficult to accept that what they are experiencing is a panic attack.

- *Disorientation.* You may wonder, How did I get here?

- *Feelings of unreality.* Even a familiar setting may look strange.

- *Heightened perception.* Things may seem too fast, too loud, or too bright.

- *Feelings of gloom and doom.* Sudden, overwhelming feelings of sadness or grief can occur.

- *Irritability.* It may be hard to cope with small irritations.

- *Dizziness.* You may feel that you're going to fall over.

- *Sweating.* A complaint is "I'm sweating, I'm ill."

- *Palpitations.* An irregular heartbeat can make it seem as though "My heart is going to burst" or "I'm having a heart attack."

- *Tight chest.* This can feel like "I can't get my breath."

- *Pain in the chest.* Chest pains* may feel like a heart attack.

- *Ringing in the ears.* This may make the head feel funny, leading to the fear of having a stroke.

- *Tingling in the hands, in the feet, or around the mouth.* This can lead to the fear that "I'm having a stroke."

- *My tongue won't work.* Slowness of the tongue can lead to the fear of having a stroke.

*Note: Pain in the chest should always be checked by a doctor.

- *I can't think of words.* This can bring on fear that "I'm having a stroke" or "I'm going senile."

- *Fainting.* When the body can't take any more adrenaline, an artificial relaxation response is produced by the brief unconsciousness caused by fainting: the muscles relax and breathing slows down.

Who Has Panic Attacks?

You, me, your neighbor, your neighbor's little girl, maybe even the pope: no one is immune. We all run on adrenaline, so therefore any one of us could suffer from a panic attack at one point or another.

Do You Have to Be an Anxious Person to Have Panic Attacks?

If you are normally anxious, you are more likely to have a panic attack than is a person who is normally relaxed. But, as you will see from the list of the causes of panic attacks, there are some physical triggers that have nothing to do with a person's usual level of anxiety.

Types of Panic Attacks

Helpful Panic Attacks

When there is real danger, say from an earthquake or an assailant, a "panic attack" is a normal response: you run away or fight. The extra adrenaline is used productively.

Unhelpful Panic Attacks

An unhelpful panic attack occurs when there is no recognizable threat: the sufferer is responding with extreme fear to a normal event, for example, standing in a line at the supermarket or going to a party. The trigger that starts a panic attack may be physical or emotional. Adrenaline floods the body to such an extent that it produces very unpleasant physical feelings, and very strong feelings of fear.

Worst of all, the sufferer does not know what to do, because he or she has no productive way to use the extra energy. A person having a panic attack might want to run screaming from the supermarket line or the party in the same way that he or she would run from an earthquake, but his or her rational mind knows that there is no real danger. It is very confusing. Unfortunately, the helpless feelings evoked by panic attacks may sow the seeds for another one, and so on.

Occasional Panic Attacks

The person who suffers occasional panic attacks finds that these attacks are often in response to specific situations, such as flying, visiting the dentist, or driving over a bridge. The attacks can also be less specific and occur when the sufferer is "run down." The attacks disappear when life is back on an even keel. Panic attacks caused by some physical triggers fall into this group. For example, a blocked nose may cause hyperventilation and panic; when breathing returns to normal, the attacks will disappear.

Panic During and After Stressful Times

For the most part, people understand when they have panic attacks during times of crisis, but they are often puzzled if the attacks do not appear until *after* a stressful event: "Jack is really well now; I'm not worried at all. Why should I have panic attacks now?" During a prolonged crisis, adrenaline levels may be raised in order to give the body more energy; these levels do not drop the instant that extra adrenaline is no longer needed. The surplus energy may discharge itself in panic attacks following the crisis.

Frequent Panic Attacks in the Nervous Person

The person who is always anxious is more likely to have panic attacks than a person who is not anxious. Life can be very limited for people who have panic attacks superimposed on a background of continuous anxiety. These people often are agoraphobic (having an abnormal fear of open spaces), and they may have social phobias as well.

People who fall into this category need professional help. However, the situation is not as bleak as it sounds. Some agoraphobics do very well. Chronic anxiety does not necessarily have to last a lifetime. Long-term reassurance and patient teaching are a vital part of treatment.

What Conditions Cause Panic Attacks?

It is somewhat arbitrary to divide the causes of panic attacks into different categories, because physical, emotional, and spiritual distress are often interwoven. I categorize the causes for ease of discussion only. We have seen that too much adrenaline can cause panic attacks, but what prompts the overproduction of this chemical? The list is quite long. (Needless to say, we will not discuss those things that would reasonably cause a panic attack, such as finding a rattlesnake in your compost pile.)

- *Physical.* For example, dieting, tight clothes, low blood pressure, inner ear problems, and so on

- *Emotional/physical.* For example, exhausted nerves, causing muscle spasm or hyperventilation (overbreathing)

- *Emotional.* For example, exhausted nerves, causing anxiety or depression

- *Spiritual.* For example, despair, no vision beyond painful reality, or death phobia

Physical Conditions

- *Dieting, fasting, and unstable blood sugar levels.* Why variations in the level of glucose in the blood cause panic attacks is fully discussed in Chapter 6.

- *Chest hugging, tight clothes, chest problems.* Any restriction in the chest can lead to hyperventilation. Hyperventilation is the chief physical cause of panic attacks.

- *Low blood pressure.* Low blood pressure can be a potent trigger for panic attacks. It can deprive the brain of oxygen, causing anxiety, dizziness, and even fainting. The opposite advice is given to people with low blood pressure than to those with high blood pressure: an increase in salt and caffeine intake and stimulation of the circulation system through exercise is suggested. In addition, an infusion of rosemary leaves (one teaspoonful of rosemary to a cup of boiling water, steep for 15 minutes, then drink half to one cup, cold, both morning and evening), or ginseng, or ginkgo bilboa are also used to elevate blood pressure. Garlic can be used to stimulate circulation.

• *Inner ear problems.* Inner ear problems can cause dizziness. It can be very frightening when the world suddenly starts to spin, particularly if it happens while you're outdoors. An attack of vertigo (a type of dizziness associated with inner ear problems) can lead to agoraphobia.

• *Allergies and side effects of drugs.* Allergic reactions and the side effects of some drugs can cause an increase in anxiety and panic attacks. Strangely enough, tranquilizers and antidepressants also can cause anxiety and panic attacks, particularly at the beginning of treatment.

• *Drug withdrawal, alcohol withdrawal, and smoking cessation.* When any drug that sedates is withdrawn, adrenaline levels rise and panic attacks can occur. (See Chapter 8.)

• *Stuffy nose.* A blocked air passage in the nose can lead to hyperventilation and panic.

• *Jet lag.* Jet lag can raise the levels of the chemical serotonin in the brain. This increase often raises anxiety levels.

• *Chronic pain.* People in pain often hyperventilate in an attempt to control their discomfort. Unfortunately, this also causes panic.

• *Injections containing adrenaline.* Some people report panic attacks after receiving a local anesthetic from the dentist. Some local anesthetics contain adrenaline.

• *Prescribed stimulant drugs.* Appetite suppressants, steroids (whether they are taken for medical purposes or to boost athletic performance), and other prescribed drugs can produce an adrenaline surge.

- *Illicit drugs.* It goes without saying that street drugs, including LSD, cocaine, and marijuana, can spawn an adrenaline rush.

- *Heat and exercise.* An overheated room can cause a panic attack, as can unaccustomed or strenuous exercise. The adrenaline levels are raised in these cases.

Emotional/Physical Conditions

- *Exhausted nerves (which then cause muscle spasm or hyperventilation), reduced activity after stressful events, hyperventilation (overbreathing), or frozen emotional pain (neurosis).* These phenomena can all lead to panic attacks.

- *Child abuse.* People who have been physically, emotionally, or sexually abused as children frequently suffer panic attacks in adult life.

Summing Up

This chapter should dispel the commonly held belief that only chronically anxious people suffer panic attacks; *anything*—physical or emotional—that dramatically increases adrenaline levels can cause a panic attack. Once you understand this phenomenon, panic attacks can be demystified and cut down to size.

CHAPTER TWO

Going to the Doctor

Treatment of Panic Attacks

The ideal treatment (although there isn't much of it around!) would be anxiety management, where you would receive counseling and learn to fully understand what is going on in your body. You would learn to retrain your breathing, receive dietary advice, learn how to cope with chronic muscle tension, and so on. In addition if your symptoms were very severe, perhaps the short-term, carefully supervised use of a tranquilizer or antidepressant could be offered.

Does Medication Help Panic Attacks?

Tranquilizers, antidepressants, and a drug called Tegretol are used for panic attacks, and some people find them helpful. Others find drugs no help at all, and many people have suffered a great deal from becoming dependent on drugs that should not be used for the long term. And it must be remembered that although these drugs can be useful for some people, in the short term they can actually be the cause of panic attacks and agoraphobia.

Does Counseling Work?

Counseling helps, but psychology alone is not enough; sufferers need to be educated about what causes their attacks. The "counseling-only" approach is not a reliable route to relief. Until the barriers of hyper-ventilation and muscle tension are broken down, the truth about a sufferer's problems can be inaccessible to both sufferer and therapist.

Compartmentalizing Medicine

In these days of one doctor for this and another doctor for that, important factors about a patient's condition frequently get overlooked. For example, once a general practitioner (GP) has referred a patient to a psychiatrist, the GP thinks his or her responsibilities are over. On the other hand, a psychiatrist who has a patient with glaring nutritional deficiencies—woefully thin, muddy skin, dull hair, and cracks at the corners of the mouth—might not notice these things because these are not psychological problems and are the province of the GP.

Through the Body to the Mind

If the holistic approach were more widely used in psychiatry, if the whole person were considered, it would change the face of modern psychiatric medicine. After more than ten years of seeing patients for whom the present system has been such a miserable failure, I feel strongly that change is needed.

I feel that the people *particularly* at risk in the system are those who have less severe (but still very distressing) symptoms of anxiety and depression (including panic attacks); people who function well enough to avoid hospital admission; and people who have had years of their lives figuratively wiped out and their anxiety problems increased by being prescribed tranquilizers. The system also fails countless others, who have their anxiety levels doubled and their own self-worth demolished by a six-week wait for a ten-minute appointment with a psychiatrist who is so rushed that the consultation must be as unrewarding for the therapist as it is unhelpful to the patient.

> I am in and out in a flash. He looks at his notes on me all the time, answers the phone, and then just says to keep on with the pills. There is so much I want to ask, but there is not enough time. I am shaking all over with anger and frustration when I come out. I usually go to the outpatient restroom for a good cry. That seems to help. I keep on thinking, Why bother going? But since this is all there is, I just keep the appointments. (*A 36-year-old lawyer*)

> I am only in for a few minutes with the psychiatrist. He asks me about the sleeping pills, and then I go for relaxation therapy. I lie down in a room, and the nurse puts a tape on. When it finishes, they come back and I go home. I don't feel this is doing much; should I continue? (*A 49-year-old unemployed steelworker*)

> He always gets my name wrong, asks if he can tape the consultation (this makes me tongue-tied, but I say yes), and then repeats the questions he asked at the last session. My sex life does not seem of great importance to me at the moment: I'm far more worried about feeling well enough to finish my degree. He does not seem to hear this. I wish he would listen. (*A 22-year-old male student*)

> I have seen both a psychiatrist and a psychologist, and neither taught me what I really wanted to know: what was actually going on in my body to give me such bizarre feelings. I have always been healthy and have very little medical awareness. I was pretty scared. I did not need to be told I had anxiety symptoms: I was living with them. I wanted to know why my hands and feet buzzed and why I felt so spaced out. I thought it must be multiple sclerosis. I would not have needed a psychiatrist if I had understood what overbreathing [hyperventilation] and not eating properly could do to

my brain. I have wasted two years of my life through their narrow-minded psychological attitude. They could only focus on my early life and fights with my boyfriend. I'm quite sure in my own mind now that the pain from the slipped disk started the habit of overbreathing, and everything stemmed from that. I feel relieved, but angry that I did not know this at the beginning. (*A 32-year-old art historian*)

How Could the System Be Improved?

What is really needed to improve the health care system for panic attack sufferers is a readily accessible nurse-therapist in the doctor's office. Not the nurse who takes temperatures and gives injections, but one who is trained in stress management; one who can get to the shoulders of tense people before they freeze, and massage them with essential oils; one whose knowledge of health education goes beyond "Stop smoking, exercise, and cut down on fat"; one who can teach deep relaxation methods; one who can reassure patients that treatment will continue until they feel confident (not "This is a stress management course that lasts six weeks"). Only then will you have a prescription many times safer and many times more effective than any prescription drug.

I am not saying that tranquilizers and sleeping pills do not have their place in the very short term: they do. But in the long term, they do a great deal more harm than good. Not only are they highly addictive for many people, but they also cause a multitude of physical and emotional problems, including depression. They also deny the patient the opportunity to learn that he or she can take charge of his or her nervous system, can regain self-esteem, and, most important, can break the cycle of panic attacks. With an anxiety management program, patients will not live in fear of another attack of "nerves," because they know that if they deal with the early signs of stress that this will not happen again, or even if they are neglectful enough to let it happen, they will have the knowledge that they can come through it the same way they did on previous occasions.

I do not believe that conventional medicine is superfluous: Western medicine and complementary medicine (for example, acupuncture, homeopathy, massage, and macrobiotics) can often work hand in hand. What I do believe is harmful is to not consider the whole organism, to put health into compartments: a pill for this part of you, cut out that offending part of you—and presto, you are cured. Dealing with the symptoms seems to be the priority of traditional Western medicine, with little thought given to the cause of the "dis-ease" and disharmony of the whole person.

Medical progress has cost us a lot, including the near extinction of the medicine woman, the old woman who lived in the woods. She was the one who would give you "opening medicine," feed you a bowl of broth, massage your aches and pains, and comfort you with wisdom that reflected her deep spirituality. This is holistic medicine. "Love is the highest level of medicine" (Paracelsus).

Will Helping Myself Work?

You can help yourself! But remember, self-help programs can be tedious. You are going to have to be prepared to make changes in your life. You will get discouraged at times, particularly if your symptoms are coming from wayward nerves, which can take time to retrain. It can also take time to restore the body to a balanced state after illness or strict dieting. *The key is to be patient.*

CHAPTER THREE

Exhausted Nerves and Panic Attacks

You will be forgiven if you say that I drone on and on about exhausted, overstimulated, or oversensitized nerves: you are quite right. I do this because to abuse the nervous system is the easiest way to disrupt your whole life. With embarrassment I admit that I do not always practice what I preach on this one, although, of late, I am trying to reform.

If you are too hard on your nerves, the adrenaline levels rise and funny (and awful) things start to happen. You are not just getting overtired and causing your muscles to ache: you are altering your brain chemistry. Inevitably, a change of mood and, personality ensue.

Imagine a picture of a violin: the strings are taut and the player is plucking the strings frenziedly. You are the player, and the taut strings are your nervous system: if you pick it, it will never get better! Sorry about the pun, but I thought this image just might make you see what you are doing to yourself. Would you kick repeatedly at a compound fracture of your lower leg?

However, raised adrenaline levels can be advantageous. This is what pushes you to win a marathon; this is what gives you extra energy to stay up late studying for finals; this is what gives you enough pep to finish your report, clean the house, weed the garden, do the ironing, and produce a perfect batch of chocolate chip cookies for a visiting relative. But when the levels of adrenaline don't fall naturally after the stressful event, and there is more stress, damage to the nerves can occur. You have to guard against the habit of unrelieved tension. You can do this only by being aware of what you are doing.

What Happens to My Body When I Am Punishing My Nerves?

PHYSICAL SIGNS OF FRAYED NERVES

The following physical signs of nerve stress show that your fight-or-flight response may be overworking.

- *Sweating.* This is usually noticeable on the palms or under the arms, but some people say that their whole body pours with sweat.

- *Palpitations.* This symptom worries most people: the heart beats wildly and seems to skip beats.

- *Digestive upsets.* The digestive system acts up with such symptoms as gas, heartburn, bloating, constipation, or diarrhea.

- *Changes in appetite.* Your desire for food changes: you either lose interest in food or you eat compulsively.

- *Urinary problems.* All bodily functions are speeded up when your nerves are frayed, including urination. There can be urgency with little warning, or a frequent need for the bathroom.

- *Blood sugar problems.* Overstimulated nerves include the nerves to the pancreas. When overstimulated, these nerves overproduce insulin. This is the opposite of, but can also be the forerunner of, diabetes. The result is increased anxiety that is often associated with hunger, panic, blurred vision, twitching in the eyelid muscles, lightheadedness, headaches, sugar craving, wanting food an hour after a heavy meal, waking in the night between 2 and 3 a.m., feelings of inner trembling with no visible shaking, cold hands and feet, and a sudden low mood. You can read more about this in Chapter 6.

- *Skin problems.* The lymphatic system (the garbage disposal system that clears out some of the waste products of metabolism) needs normal muscular action to function properly. If you are stiff and tense, toxins cannot be eliminated successfully through the skin, and pimples and acne are the result.

CHRONIC MUSCLE SPASM

Chronic muscle spasm can lead to the following problems:

- *Headaches.* Tension in the scalp is the cause of the common tight-band headache. Neck and shoulder tension can cause a dull ache around the base of the skull, and a feeling of being only partially present or depressed.

- *Neck and shoulder tension.* The neck is the pathway to the head. If the neck and shoulder muscles are tight, the circulation to the head is restricted. It's like putting a tight cord around your neck. This can cause the following:

  Dizziness
  Ringing in the ears
  Blurred vision
  Sinus problems

- *Backaches.* When the muscles on the sides of the neck are tense, the position of the head is altered. This transfers the tension all the way down the spine, resulting in back problems.

- *Wobbly legs.* If the spine is out of alignment, the legs do not work properly and you feel as if your legs can't hold you up.

- *Shaking.* When the body is geared for action and the action is not taken, shaking often occurs. Shaking expends unused energy.

- *Tight chest.* When the chest feels tight, it is usually the result of overbreathing (see Chapter 4).

- *Loss of interest in sex.* Every system in the body can be disrupted by frayed nerves, so it would be surprising if the hormones were not affected. In addition, with so much energy going into tension, and the body trying to balance on a spine that is being pulled in all directions, there may not be enough energy left for sex. Fear also causes loss of libido.

- *Insomnia.* When you understand what is going on in your body, you will see that insomnia is an inevitable physiological result of what you are doing to your body and mind during the day. Like panic attacks, insomnia is not a mysterious condition over which you have no control.

EMOTIONAL SIGNS OF FRAYED NERVES

- *Irritability.* Irritability is a sign of being overstressed and means being annoyed by things that would not normally bother you, such as the line at the bank moving slowly, the package of crackers that refuses to open without scissors, a teasing remark (even from a loved one), or a wrong telephone number.

- *Confusion.* You know that you may be in trouble when you find yourself asking, Have I given the cat his pill? Yes, I have; no I haven't, or you forget telephone numbers you have known for years, or you buy a newspaper you already bought earlier in the day.

- *Restlessness.* Feeling uncomfortable with your present circumstances can be a symptom of frayed nerves. If you're inside, you want to be outside; if you're outside, you want to be inside.

- *Hyperactivity.* You find yourself doing several things at once at top speed.

- *Lack of concentration.* Mental tasks you have always found simple seem to be hard to focus on.

- *Rapid speech.* You can hear yourself going on and on, but you can't seem to control it.

- *Rapid thoughts.* Your mind is like a grasshopper, jumping from one thing to the next. The same line of a song runs through your head all day and into the night.

- *Paranoia.* You feel that people don't like you or are talking about you. Your self-esteem is very low: you don't like yourself much at the moment. (Perhaps that's why you think others don't like you.)

- *Phobias.* You are afraid of things that do not normally worry you, such as going shopping, staying in a strange place, or crossing a bridge.

- *Feelings of gloom and doom.* Morbid thoughts preoccupy you; you know they are silly but they still come.

- *Crying easily.* You burst into tears when you bang your elbow, hear a sudden noise, or even read a particular sentence in a book. Your emotions surface easily.

- *Fainting.* Your body may discharge pent-up energy in a fearful or emotionally charged situation by fainting.

How Have I Gotten Myself into This State?

Panic attacks often occur when you have ignored your basic needs, either by pushing your body or mind too far or by not listening to your inner being (your soul, your spirit, or whatever you call your essence). Or perhaps you have done all of these things.

PHYSICALLY PUNISHING YOURSELF

Do you push yourself to work just that extra half hour, and then that extra half-hour becomes an hour? Do you ignore how you sit or stand? Do you fail to take frequent breaks from your working position and from repetitive movements? Do you have quick fixes—coffee, tea, cigarettes, chocolate, alcohol, or drugs—instead of well-spaced regular meals? Do you breathe just enough to prevent yourself from fainting? Do you continually take on more than you can reasonably cope with? Are you incapable of seeing your own needs and saying no? Do you deprive yourself of fresh air, light, and exercise?

BRAIN FATIGUE

Brain fatigue is a condition characterized by confused thinking, a lack of interest in life, and weariness. The brain is like any other part of the body: if you use it too much, it becomes fatigued. Constant worry, overwork, lack of sleep, or never giving your brain a rest produces fatigue. Can you ever just "be" and do nothing at all? Or do you imagine you are resting if you merely sit in an easy chair away from your workplace: "I'll just look at this report"; "I'll just write . . ."; "I'll just mend." Do you ever give your mind some time off, to repair, to drift? Or are you afraid to stop?

SOUL STARVATION

One thing we tend to ignore in our lives is the care of our souls. Do you ignore promptings from your higher self: your intuitive knowledge, or the guidance of your dreams? Do you deny your spirituality? Do you confuse religion and spirituality, and dismiss them both? I will offer more about paying attention to your inner being in later chapters.

Summing up

In this chapter, we have discussed some of the causes of panic attacks. You can see that the most common cause is exhausted nerves. Very much associated with this condition is overbreathing, or hyperventilation. We will discuss this more in Chapter 4.

CHAPTER FOUR

Half-Breathe, Half-Live

Panic Attacks and Overbreathing

This is a happy chapter. You are not going to get dreary statistics. I'm not going to shout, "Death to chocolate cake!" I am merely going to explain how poor breathing habits not only can make you feel dizzy and slightly unwell, but also how they can cause severe symptoms (including panic attacks) that can mimic many known diseases, often resulting in misdiagnosis.

The effects of overbreathing range from feeling a little dizzy, being "spaced out," having a tight throat or bloated abdomen, to suffering severe chest pain. Other outcomes include panic attacks, feeling unreal, anxiety, depression, and muscle and joint pains. Overbreathing, or hyperventilation, can also complicate the picture when there is known organic disease. So you can see that hyperventilation is an important subject. From 6 to 11 percent of all patients seen in general practice breathe in this unhealthy manner.

Calming the Breath to Control Hyperventilation

I thought it would be less confusing to include this simple way of breathing here rather than with the breathing exercises described in Chapter 9. Learning this elementary method is the first step to overcoming hyperventilation and panic attacks.

The principle is very simple. All you have to do is to make your "out" breath longer than your "in" breath.

1. Breathe in quickly but gently (preferably through the nose), for a count of 2 or 3. Do not take deep, gulping breaths. Do not hold your breath.

2. Breathe out gently, letting your jaw go slack, to a count of 4 or 6. Do not blow out hard or force it.

After a few weeks' practice you can make the "out" breath even longer, and keep a gentle rhythm going: "in" 1, 2 , 3; "out" 1, 2, 3, 4, 5, 6, 7, 8, 9. Take it easy: it takes time to get to this stage. You will soon start to feel in control of yourself by using this simple method. (This yoga breath [pranayama] is recommended for the control of hyperventilation symptoms.)

What Is Overbreathing?

Overbreathing is simply breathing in excess of the body's requirements. It is characterized by rapid respirations from the upper chest, with marked variations in the rhythm and rate, often accompanied by frequent sighing or the need to take an occasional deep breath. It is sometimes called shoulder breathing. Because such a small amount of the lung capacity is being used, the breathing pattern produces changes in carbon dioxide levels in the blood, seriously disrupting the functioning of the nervous system. The resulting disturbance in brain chemistry alters perceptions, and sufferers are unable to make sense of what they see and hear. The consequences of overbreathing can be bizarre, and are often so frightening that they trigger further panic attacks. Even if the neurological effects caused by a fall in the carbon dioxide levels are not severe enough to cause panic attacks, the continuous stress on the nervous system can lead to nervous exhaustion.

What Causes Overbreathing?

Anxiety, anything that constricts the chest (such as tight clothing or a cramped posture), a stuffy nose, and chronic muscular tension are all major causes of overbreathing. Other factors can be gas in the stomach or bowel, pain, excitement, compulsive talking, fear, a deficiency of B vitamins, a poor nutritional state, or a diet high in sugar.

- *Anxiety*
  It is natural for the breathing to speed up when we need action. When we are anxious, the breathing mechanism is always in a state halfway to red alert.

- *Constriction of the chest*
  Anything that does not allow full expansion of the chest, such as tight clothing, muscle tension, poor posture, working in a confined space, or broken ribs, can cause overbreathing.

- *Breathing difficulties*
  Some chest conditions, such as pleurisy or upper respiratory problems that cause a blocked nose, make the sufferer take small breaths through the mouth, creating difficulties.

- *Chronic muscular tension*
  This is a very important cause of overbreathing. Not only are the respiratory muscles—the diaphragm and chest muscles—involved, but the sternomastoid muscles are also implicated. (One end of the sternomastoid runs from behind the ear to the upper end of the breastbone, and the other end runs from the collarbone to the base of the skull.) The sternomastoid muscles help to lift the collarbones and breastbones and are an important part of the breathing mechanism. In Chapter 11, you will see why it is important to avoid tension in these muscles. If the sternomastoid muscles cannot rest at full length, the tension can cause ear, sinus, throat, and allergy problems, in addition to affecting breathing.

Can Overbreathing Be Corrected?

The symptoms caused by overbreathing, or hyperventilation, disappear when normal breathing patterns are established. (More about this later.)

When you read the list of symptoms caused by overbreathing, you will see that many of them are identical to those of a panic attack. I can hear you saying, I can understand a soldier in combat being so afraid that he overbreathes enough to have a panic attack, but I shouldn't be afraid while I'm in the supermarket. Why does it happen to me? How can I be hyperventilating? The answer is that if the fear comes from your subconscious, you may not be able to make sense of it. If you repeatedly have the same response to the same situation, you may have to accept that something is triggering your fear, causing you to overbreathe and then panic.

Do Many People Know about Overbreathing?

As a result of articles in the popular press, public awareness is growing. On the other hand, medical awareness, unfortunately, is still in its infancy. Few doctors notice the subtle, but extremely common, symptom picture of the low-grade, habitual hyperventilator. They are only aware of severe symptoms (difficulty breathing and tetany, a clawlike muscle spasm of the hands) of overt hyperventilation. Why is this so? Is it because the subject is given little importance in medical curricula? Is it because the symptoms mimic so many conditions and medical practitioners are always looking for organic disease? Or is it that the ever-handy diagnoses of anxiety or depression conveniently solve the problem, and the tranquilizers or antidepressants often prescribed coincidentally relieve some of the symptoms?

It could be that some doctors feel that this subject is "old hat" and skip over the coverage in medical journals, or perhaps documentation on the subject has been around too long. Whatever the reason, judging by the number of people who undergo unnecessary neurological, cardiac, and respiratory examinations, hyperventilation is a condition that is repeatedly overlooked. This is too bad, because a simple test—the provocation test—in which patients are asked to overbreathe for two to three minutes, can confirm the diagnosis of hyperventilation. The symptoms are then compared with those experienced during a panic attack. This test could relieve a lot of anxiety and save a lot of money. Doctors are often as baffled as their patients by the strange symptoms, but do not consider hyperventilation as a cause. It is rare for patients to be taught breathing retraining by their physicians. It can be done, and it would cut down the need for prescriptions for tranquilizers and antidepressants.

Is It Difficult to Spot the Chronic Hyperventilator?

To be fair, the chronic hyperventilator often does have the symptoms of anxiety and depression, but this still cannot excuse the frequency with which the clear physical manifestations of hyperventilation are missed.

The Chicken or the Egg?

Which comes first? Does hyperventilation cause anxiety symptoms, or does anxiety cause hyperventilation symptoms? It would appear by the dearth of treatment for overbreathing that most practitioners accept the latter, although L. C. Lum, M.D., an expert on this subject, holds the opposite view.

Educating Overbreathers

The first step in helping people who hyperventilate is to convince them that their symptoms are coming from shallow breathing. This is often not an easy task. Some sufferers dismiss the suggestion as being too simple an answer to their problems, and others are wary, feeling that they are being blamed. People need to be reassured that breathing in excess of the body's requirements produces a complex chain of physiological events that can disrupt many systems in the body. If sufferers argue that they don't normally breathe at the rate of the provocation test it should be explained to them that even two breaths per minute more than the body needs can produce symptoms.

When a sufferer feels that he or she is being accused of hysterical hyperventilation, it is useful to explain that it would be hard to hysterically hyperventilate during sleep, which many people do, and that is why it is possible to wake up with a panic attack.

Once people are convinced that overbreathing is causing their symptoms (this may take more than one provocation test), they are taught to respond to stress with slow breathing. Breathing retraining is an important factor in treatment. However, the retraining often takes weeks of tedious effort. (For breathing exercises, see Chapter 9.)

To tell a patient that there is nothing organically wrong with him or her may, paradoxically, cause more anxiety. The patient may conclude that they have some serious complaints that defy diagnosis, or that the doctor believes that they are imagining the symptoms.

The Aim of This Chapter

Some of the effects of overbreathing are bizarre. A very frightened person often inquires, "Am I having a stroke? I have this strange tingling in my hands and feet. It's in my mouth, too. My lips are stiff and tingly, and my tongue feels too big; it makes it difficult to form some words."

This chapter explains the symptoms of hyperventilation and suggests some reasons why so many of us have become hyperventilators. It discusses how an alteration in the acid–alkaline balance of the blood produced by overbreathing can affect the smooth running of every system in the body.

Do-it-yourself diagnosis can be very dangerous; it is therefore essential to consult your doctor about any medical problem. If you have been told that there is nothing wrong and still feel below par, compare your symptom picture with that of a chronic hyperventilator. If it looks familiar, start working on the practical self-help program. Even if you are unsure, try the suggestions. Taking another look at yourself, and trying to improve your general health is always worthwhile.

Symptoms of Overbreathing

- *Anxiety.* A state of constant fear.

- *Panic attacks.* Disabling episodes of fear, lasting minutes or hours.

- *Depression.* Loss of interest in life; illness of the spirit.

- *Feelings of unreality.* Altered perception, causing the familiar to seem unfamiliar.

- *Sense of hopelessness.* Despair; little sense of joy.

- *Poor memory.* Tension causes poor concentration, so that a person cannot recall a familiar name or what he or she had for breakfast.

- *Agoraphobia.* A fear of open spaces.

- *Other phobias.* Sudden strong fear of everyday things, such as social events, water, or buttons.

- *Palpitations.* Rapid heartbeat, missed heartbeats, or a sensation of fluttering in the chest.

- *Shortness of breath.* The inability to take deep breaths. Frequent sighing: 80 percent of the patients who hyperventilate sigh often.

- *Dry throat.* Clearing the throat, or moistening dry lips.

- *Dry cough.* This is due to water and heat loss from the mucosal lining of the airway.

- *Stuffy nose.* Symptoms include dryness in the nose, sores in the nose, and sniffing.

- *Chest pain.* Either a sharp pain lasting seconds or minutes, or a dull ache over the heart and around the breastbone and ribs. This pain is caused by the strain on the muscles and ligaments from continually breathing from the upper chest. Finger pressure around the breastbone or ribs can locate very sore spots. There is also an inability to lie on the left side. The pain is not usually affected by breathing. It can occur after exercise. Pressure from gas in the stomach can also cause chest pain. Spasm in the coronary artery can cause severe chest pain, and people often arrive at the emergency room (sometimes several times a year) complaining of this. Chest pain does not usually appear with the provocation test.

- *Yawning.* Air hunger.

- *Lightheadedness and dizziness.* These are the most common symptoms.

- *Feeling of impending fainting.* This affects all ages.

- *Actual fainting.* This is more common in the young.

- *Tingling.* This can occur in the hands, feet, or around the mouth.

- *Weakness.* This can occur in all the muscles.

- *Numbness.* This can be anywhere in the body.

- *Jelly legs.* A feeling that the legs cannot support the body.

- *Digestive disturbances.* Heartburn, bloating, belching, gas in the bowel, air swallowing, food intolerance, or irritable bowel syndrome.

- *Muscle spasm.* Particularly in the neck and shoulders. Claw-like spasm in the hands and feet (tetany).

- *Speech difficulties.* Feeling of the tongue being swollen.

- *Hallucinations.* This occurs only when symptoms are severe. (The connection between hyperventilation and hallucinations is seen in a playground game among children: they take gulping breaths and are spun around by their peers in order to get dizzy and "see pictures.")

Case Studies

James was a 62-year-old retired real estate agent. He was a cheerful man and did not seem particularly anxious, although his symptoms were beginning to restrict his activities. He was often lightheaded and dizzy, and occasionally he fainted. James had undergone a complete series of hospital tests, including an angiogram (to see that the blood supply to his head was not obstructed). All the tests were negative, but the symptoms persisted. Often when patients have a long list of symptoms, they relate only a few of them to their doctor because they feel foolish: they usually mention only the ones that cause them the most distress. So when James finally said that he had difficulty taking a deep breath, had tingling in the hands and around the mouth, and was more tired than usual, the diagnosis of chronic hyperventilation was made. His symptoms disappeared after breathing retraining, and on the occasions when he felt a slight attack coming on, he was able to ward off the symptoms by bag rebreathing. (See page 76.)

Martin was a hard-working, conscientious man of 36. He had never had any anxiety problems and was physically strong. He described his panic attacks as the most bewildering thing that had ever happened to him.

> The first one came when I was bending over, weeding the garden. My chest felt tight and my heart was beating so strongly that I felt I must be having a heart attack. Everything seemed unreal: the flowers looked so bright and the noise from a lawn mower several gardens away seemed deafening. I was very scared: perspiration was pouring out of me, and my arms and legs felt as though they did not belong to me. I made myself walk around and the feelings began to ease, although I was still very shaken. My wife later said that I had been a shade of pale gray. She gave me some sweet tea, and this seemed to release an enormous amount of gas from my stomach.

> The second attack came a few weeks later when I was cleaning the inside of the car. This time I was convinced that I had something wrong with my heart and called the emergency doctor. He said that it was just anxiety and suggested a warm bath, some peppermint for the gas, and an early night. He seemed to take it so lightly: I was annoyed and far from convinced that there was nothing seriously wrong. I saw my own doctor the next day. He also confirmed that there was nothing physically wrong and started to ask questions about my lifestyle. I have to confess that I felt annoyed once again,

but as he explained things I began to see a pattern: on each occasion I had hurried a big meal, and then worked in a crouched position. I also had to admit that I had been working longer hours and losing sleep since the baby arrived. It's quite hard to be told to slow down when you're only 36.

Martin's symptoms suggest that excess gas in his stomach pushed up on his lungs and triggered hyperventilation, which caused his panic attacks. In view of the way he had been overtiring himself, it is probable that he had been hyperventilating to some degree for some time without noticing it. The extra trigger was enough to produce the severe symptoms.

At 57, Maria felt depressed and hopeless. Her symptoms were numbness, tingling, dizziness, anxiety, palpitations, inability to take a deep breath, and a sensation that she had a lump in her throat. She also had a persistent feeling that something awful was about to happen. A six-week stay in a psychiatric hospital, where she underwent psychotherapy and was treated with antidepressants, failed to relieve her symptoms.

Her story illustrates how a person's physical symptoms (clearly manifestations of hyperventilation) can be discounted. Maria began to feel a gulf between herself and the people close to her because of their lack of understanding about her illness. Maria's symptoms responded quite quickly to bag rebreathing, which impressed her. Her sister participated in her sessions, and she, too, was enthusiastic. Maria worked hard at her breathing exercises, and within three weeks she had greatly reduced her symptoms.

Louise had severe symptoms, including blackouts, and was understandably very frightened. She had her symptoms analyzed by a physician and was informed that she was a chronic hyperventilator. Unfortunately, she was not given any real help, but was simply instructed to slow down her breathing. Convinced that she was suffering from something much more serious, Louise didn't take this diagnosis seriously. She continued to feel miserable, experiencing tingling and numbness around her mouth and in her hands. Foods that had not upset her in the past began to cause discomfort, and she soon lost interest in eating. Around midafternoon her abdomen would start to swell, and by evening she would be very bloated and uncomfortable. Her energy level was low.

Feeling that Louise was not trying to help herself, her husband lost patience with her. To please him, she went to an anxiety management group. When she saw that others had the same symptoms, she was encouraged. If she used bag rebreathing as soon as the tingling and numbness began, she could avoid a blackout, giving her more self-confidence. (Some people say that they realize they had the tingling for years before the blackouts developed.) After several months, Louise was still anxious, but much improved. Eating without subsequent discomfort was still a problem, but otherwise she was leading a normal life.

Julie had never been an anxious person. She enjoyed her work and had a full social life. She went to her doctor because she was experiencing "horrible feelings" upon waking, and during other times of the day. These sensations had come on suddenly, causing her to feel distressed and very puzzled. She thought she must be developing asthma, because she was finding it difficult to take a deep breath. She also complained of dizziness, and although she had not actually fainted, she often felt that she was about to collapse.

Julie's doctor reassured her that she did not have asthma and confirmed that she was physically fit. When he asked if she was anxious about anything, she said no. He pointed out that her pulse and breathing were rather rapid for someone who was not feeling anxious. She said that her mother had commented several weeks earlier that her breathing was "funny." This had occurred about eight weeks after she had cracked two ribs when she slipped by a swimming pool. Her physician had not known about this accident, as she had been on vacation at the time. When she mentioned the accident to her doctor, things began to make sense to him. He concluded that she must have started to overbreathe to avoid the pain caused by the accident, and that the habit had persisted after her ribs had healed. This explanation made sense to Julie. She started to breathe from her abdomen and joined a yoga class. Daytime symptoms were easily controlled with correct breathing, but it took longer for the early morning symptoms to disappear: Julie was obviously still over-breathing in her sleep. She found that lying flatter helped (she had used more pillows since she had cracked her ribs), as did sleeping with a sheet over her face. (This technique gives you back some of the carbon dioxide you lose when you breathe.)

John was very scared by his first panic attack and wasted no time in seeing a doctor. It was really no surprise to him: he had been waiting for something to happen, because, by his own admission, he had been burning the candle at both ends. He also admitted that he had been dabbling in street drugs for several months: speed and cocaine. One day, while he was waiting for a dryer at the laundromat, he suddenly felt as if he could not swallow. He became so frightened that he thought he would pass out. For several months, there had been warning signs—his pulse would race and his thoughts would be jumbled—but he had ignored them. Because of the severity of the panic attacks, John lost all interest in drugs. He took two weeks' rest and ate regular meals. His panic attacks stopped.

Children and Hyperventilation

Rapid overbreathing is common in childhood, and can be an indica-tion that a child is under severe strain. A study reviewing the records of 34 children younger than 18 who had been seen at the Mayo Clinic in a 25-year period found that up to 40 percent were still hyperventilating as adults, and many suffered from chronic anxiety and depression. Symptoms included headaches, frequent vomiting, irritable bowel, phobias, eye blinking, nail biting, and bed wetting.

Treatment

Professional help should be sought for the child who is hyperventi-lating, unless it is an isolated incident after a cold or fright. A minor-ity of children who hyperventilate hysterically may be using the behavior to manipulate the adults around them, but in any case this behavior should be analyzed and not ignored.

Breathing Retraining for Children

Retraining a child to breathe properly can be made into a game. Coloring or making the rebreathing paper bag into a cartoon character can be fun. Singing, playing wind instruments, and swimming also encourage the child to use his or her lungs to full capacity. It is essential, of course, that the cause of stress in the child's life be investigated and, as much as possible, eliminated. (Medical references on hyperventilation follow in Chapter 5.)

What Can I Do about My Overbreathing?

If you cannot get professional help, practice the exercises in Chapter 9 daily. To control a panic attack, you should first correct your breathing. Then you should ask yourself, When did I last eat? The importance of proper eating is described in detail in Chapter 6.

CHAPTER FIVE

Hyperventilation—
Some Medical Evidence

Hyperventilation was first documented in 1871 by Jacob Mendez Da Costa, M.D. During the Civil War, he observed 300 soldiers with a strange illness: the men were out of breath, tired, and dizzy, and they complained of heart palpitations and pain in the chest. They also complained of headaches and disturbed sleep. In spite of all these symptoms, Da Costa noted that the men did not have fevers and were otherwise well. The treatment was removal from active duty and rest, but even with this regimen he noted that "the irritability of the heart remained," and only slowly did the heart return to normal. Da Costa did not associate these symptoms with over-breathing, but he did realize that he had seen the same symptoms in his private practice.

The syndrome (a collection of symptoms) was called Da Costa's syndrome or irritable heart. It was noticed again during World War I, and was renamed soldiers' heart or effort syndrome. These terms were rejected by American medical officers, because they feared that the soldiers would believe that they had a heart condition. (A great many people who have panic attacks cannot be convinced that they have healthy hearts). The syndrome was then called neurocirculatory asthenia. It would have been more straightforward, of course, to call it the scared soldier syndrome! (Sadly, it seems that fighting men were not allowed to feel afraid.)

The following is an excerpt from an article in a medical journal. You should find it very comforting. I have italicized the good news. (Don't be put off by dates and reference numbers: what is being said is really very exciting.)

> It is often assumed that anxiety is the chief, or only cause of hyperventilation. On the contrary, any change of mood—happiness, laughter, relief, animated conversation and even watching television—can frequently be the cause. The first attacks commonly follow a purely physical illness. General anesthesia and operations are potent triggers. The driving personality, addicted to his work, often develops the first attack at weekends or on holiday. Anxiety then develops out of the persistent symptoms. With repetition the response takes on the character of a conditioned reflex (Cannon 1928).

> Although Kerr et al. (1937) had pointed out that the clinical manifestations of anxiety state were produced by hyperventilation, it was Rice (1950) who turned this concept upside down by stating that *patients could be cured by eliminating faulty breathing habits*. Lewis (1964) identified the role of anxiety as a trigger rather than the prime cause. Given habitual hyperventilation, a variety of triggers, psychic or somatic, can initiate the vicious cycle of increased breathing, symptoms, and anxiety arising from exacerbating hyperventilation, thus generating more symptoms and more anxiety. He claimed a 70 percent cure rate by breathing re-education. ("Hyperventilation Syndromes in Medicine and Psychiatry: A Review," by L. C. Lum, M.D., *Journal of the Royal Society of Medicine* 80 [1987], p. 229.)

Here is another excerpt which discusses all the familiar symptoms of hyperventilation. It is from the *Oxford Textbook of Psychiatry* (1983):

> Overbreathing is breathing in a rapid and shallow way which results in a fall of the concentration of carbon dioxide in the blood. The resultant symptoms include dizziness, faintness, numbness and tingling in the hands, feet, and face, carpopedal spasms [severe cramp in hands and feet], and precordial discomfort [area of the chest over the heart]. There is also a feeling of breathlessness which may prolong the condition. When a patient has unexplained bodily symptoms, the possibility of persistent overbreathing should always be born in mind.

The following excerpt from another article shows that one of the major causes of panic attacks is simply incorrect breathing.

> The syndrome (collection of symptoms) characterized by repeated panic attacks has been known by several names including muscular exhaustion of the heart, neurasthenia (nervous exhaustion), irritable heart, anxiety neurosis, effort syndrome, and cardiac neurosis. The manual's definition of panic disorder states that attacks are manifested by the sudden onset of intense apprehension, fear, or terror, often associated with feelings of impending doom. The most common symptoms experienced during an attack are dyspnoea [difficulty breathing], choking or smothering sensation, dizziness, vertigo, or unsteady feelings, feelings of unreality, paraesthesias [disordered sensation, such as tingling or pins and needles], hot and cold flushes, sweating, faintness, trembling or shaking, and fear of dying, going crazy, or doing something uncontrolled during the attack. Attacks usually last minutes; more rarely hours. ("Hyperventilation [Shallow Breathing] as a Cause of Panic Attacks," by G. A. Hibbert, M.D., *British Medical Journal* 288, January 28, 1984.)

CHAPTER SIX

Hypoglycemia: Low Blood Sugar

After I explain the term *hypoglycemia*, I will use the term *unstable blood sugar levels*, because this more accurately describes what is about to be discussed. *Hypo* means "low," and *glycemia* means "blood sugar," so this term simply means "a low level of sugar (glucose) in the blood." *Hyper* means "high," so *hyperglycemia* means "a high level of sugar in the blood."

You might wonder why there is so much talk of low blood sugar when most people eat too much sugar. You might also question why people with two apparently opposite conditions—low blood sugar and diabetes—have similar diets. The person with low blood sugar cuts down on sugar to stop the overproduction of insulin. Diabetics cut down on sugar because their bodies do not produce enough insulin to metabolize the sugar.

Do We Need Sugar at All?

We don't need sugar in the form of simple (refined) carbohydrates, which have mostly empty calories: calories without nutrients. What we do need are complex, (unrefined) carbohydrates: whole grains, fruits, and vegetables. These have good food value and can also be broken down slowly by the digestive system before being passed into the blood as glucose. Sucrose—sweets, white flour, and so on— are simple, refined carbohydrates. No sooner are they in the mouth than, presto, they are in the blood. They give the pancreas quite a jolt. (The pancreas is the organ that produces the insulin necessary for the body to function properly.)

Low Blood Sugar and the Medical Profession

The medical controversy about low blood sugar, or hypoglycemia, rages. Comments range from the American Medical Association's, "It [hypoglycemia] is very common. It just managed to avoid publicity" to Vincent Marks in the *London Times*, November 1983, expressing his worries over "this newly fashionable condition" that might provide fringe practitioners with business opportunities. Is it really just a current vogue? Medical interest started in the 1920s and S. Soskin, in the *Journal of Clinical Endocrinology and Metabolism* (1944) states that "Hyperglycemia (high blood sugar) does not represent nearly so immediate a threat to the well-being of the body as does hypoglycemia." This statement is even stronger when you consider that a person with diabetes (hyperglycemia) will be diagnosed and treated correctly, whereas the person with hypoglycemia is unlikely to be correctly diagnosed, can be subjected to countless tests, and may even be given years of drugs (usually tranquilizers), that worsen the condition. Alternatively, sufferers may be told that they are "just anxious" or malingering; the symptoms may go untreated and they may have years of misery.

It cannot be argued that too much insulin does not cause symptoms, because the patient who has had stomach surgery or the nondiabetic patient who is given insulin has the same symptom picture as the person with overstimulated nerves who is overproducing insulin.

There Is a Lot of Hypoglycemia Around

Perhaps the truth is that since the beginning of the century, the incidence of hypoglycemia has risen along with many other conditions, including cancer. But because the symptoms of cancer can be observed and treated with drugs or surgery, they are viewed rather differently. Because most of the symptoms of low blood sugar affect the brain (we will see why later), it is easy for medical practitioners to declare that patients are neurotic or overly imaginative.

The medical profession can be quite narrowminded when they don't *expect* the human body to react in a certain way. The case of the benzodiazepines proves this point. Millions of people worldwide became pharmacologically dependent on tranquilizers such as Valium (diazepam), Ativan (lorazepam), and sleeping pills such as temazepam and nitrazepam. The medical profession did not see the problem because they did not expect it.

Why Is There a Lot of Hypoglycemia Around?

When human beings and medical science become careless about how they treat the human body, the body is bound to become less efficient. Mechanisms that *should* not go wrong, do. What have we done?

- *Changes in Diet*

  Think about what has happened to our eating patterns during this century. Once we lived on a diet of whole grains, abundant vegetables, meat, poultry, fish, and honey; now we eat enormous quantities of sugar, grains that have had the nutrients knocked out of them, and animal products that are contaminated with hormones and antibiotics.

  What ever happened to the stockpot? It's been a long time since a broth of beans and vegetables was the mainstay of the diet, and plates were piled high with greens, baked potatoes, and carrots. A small salad next to a hamburger and fries seems to be the norm these days.

- *The Pace of Life*

  People run around in all directions, with little time to prepare or eat wholesome food. A scant breakfast is followed by a rushed lunch, and the family meal is often what a harassed parent can pick up in the way of fast food on the way home from work. The time taken to eat may depend on what is showing on television. Are there many families whose members talk to each other in a leisurely fashion over wholesome food? You will see later the positive effect of unhurried, well-spaced meals.

- *Prescribed Drugs and Blood Sugar Problems*
  If a change of diet is the first cause of low blood sugar problems in modern men and women, then pills for all ills must be the second. Medical evidence has clearly shown that contraceptive pills, steroids, tranquilizers, sleeping pills, beta blockers, and some diuretics (pills to relieve water retention) affect glucose intolerance, cholesterol, and triglyceride metabolism. These adverse reactions often go unnoticed because they are not dramatic. The onset of low blood sugar is insidious, and is often not understood to be associated with prescribed drugs, either by the doctor or the patient.

- *Increase in the Use of Nonprescribed Drugs*
  Alcohol, tobacco, tea, coffee, cola, and street drugs— including heroin, cocaine, and marijuana—all affect blood sugar levels.

I Have Low Blood Sugar: Should I Go to the Doctor?

Unless you feel that you have developed low blood sugar symptoms since you have been on a prescribed drug, it is probably a waste of time to go the doctor. My experience with the reaction by the general medical community to this problem is: "Yes, it is hypoglycemia: drink sweet tea!" or "No, only diabetics develop low blood sugar from their prescribed medication. You are just anxious."

Does Keeping Blood Sugar Levels Stable Really Help?

My belief is that it very definitely does. I have seen hypoglycemia in a clinical setting on a diabetic ward, and also in the community while working with people with anxiety problems. In the latter group, perhaps the condition could more accurately be called unstable blood sugar levels, rather than low blood sugar levels, because symptoms can occur when the blood sugar levels are within normal limits. It appears that it's the sudden drops in blood sugar levels that cause the problems, rather than the blood sugar levels being abnormally low. It is interesting to note that blood taken while patients were actually having panic attacks showed sugar levels on the lower end of the scale, but never actually below normal, yet patients' symptoms responded dramatically to a diet designed to keep blood sugar levels stable.

After seeing hundreds of people improve when following a low blood sugar eating plan (which needs to be a lot more than just sensible eating), I have concluded that diet plays a large part in the management of not only anxiety, but also migraine headaches, premenstrual syndrome (PMS), and some types of asthma. Although I see diet as an important part of treatment, I also feel strongly that the approach to it should be one of common sense rather than rigidity.

SHOULD I HAVE A BLOOD SUGAR TEST?

The blood sugar test, called a glucose tolerance test, involves testing blood and urine specimens every half hour for several hours while consuming a measured amount of glucose. The test, unfortunately, can also also make the patient feel ill for several days.

I see the answer as simple: if the symptoms are coming from unstable blood sugar levels, then they will respond to diet within a few days; if they are not, then there is no blood sugar problem.

In my work in the community throughout the past ten years, it has been my great joy to see so many "no breakfast, sandwich lunch, large evening meal" eaters reduce their adrenaline levels, lose many of their anxiety symptoms, and become confident and in charge of their health by simply stopping their blood sugar levels from bouncing up and down ("kangarooing").

IT'S YOUR BODY

I never cease to marvel at the accuracy of people's intuitive feelings about what ails their bodies. If you feel that your symptom picture fits with the symptoms that follow, heed the recommendations. You have nothing to lose. Do remember that the condition brought about by unstable blood sugar levels is not an illness, but merely a result of stress and an incorrect diet.

Symptoms of Unstable Blood Sugar Levels

Many of the anxiety symptoms discussed in the preceding chapters also appear when the blood sugar drops quickly, so I will not cover them again in detail. We have seen that when the body is under stress, circulation is affected, resulting in heart palpitations, missed heartbeats, and so on. In addition to these symptoms, there are some that are more specific to changing blood sugar levels. These include dull headaches, inner trembling with no visible shaking, sugar craving, low energy in the midmorning and midafternoon, twitching eyelid muscles, wanting to eat again about an hour after the evening meal, no desire for breakfast, lapses in concentration, tenderness over the pancreas area, sore trigger points over the left lower ribs, and awaking between 3 and 5 a.m., alert, anxious and sometimes hungry.

ADRENAL EXHAUSTION: NERVOUS EXHAUSTION

When blood sugar levels drop, the adrenal glands, located above the kidneys, produce cortisone and adrenaline to make the glucose stored in the liver available for use. When these glands are continually taxed, the condition known as adrenal exhaustion follows: the body is no longer able to deal with stress. Anxiety, panic attacks, depression, irritability, and an eventual change of personality can arise from the nerve cells being continually deprived of nourishment.

UNSTABLE BLOOD SUGAR LEVELS AND PANIC ATTACKS

You can now understand why a dramatic drop in blood sugar levels causes a flood of adrenaline. Why this is such a potent trigger for a panic attack is explained on pages 45–46.

CAUTION: PAY ATTENTION!

Many of my readers (including my clients) have confessed that they have skipped the chapter on blood sugar levels in my books, thinking that I was talking vaguely about nutrition. It was not until they heard me teach (or perhaps preach would be a better word) that they understood the full implications of the subject. When people fully comprehend what is involved, and how dietary neglect hurts their nervous system, they are much more willing to follow the rules.

What Happens When I Don't Eat Properly?

Sugar is an important constituent of the body. Having been converted from the food we eat, sugar is carried into the bloodstream in the form of glucose. Any excess sugar is stored in the liver as glycogen, and it is this store that we call on when there is no food left in the digestive tract. We do not need large quantities of sugar to keep this supply of glucose steady, because most foods, with the exception of fats, can be turned into glucose. Proteins (meat, fish, dairy products, nuts, seeds, and legumes) are converted by the liver into glucose, but this happens only when the bowel is empty of carbohydrates (sugar, bread, cakes, pastas, potatoes, rice, cereals, fruit, or vegetables).

BRAIN FOOD

Glucose is the body's fuel. The brain is totally dependent on this form of food: without it, it would die. This is important to remember when looking at the list of symptoms caused by unstable blood sugar levels. The brain cannot utilize other foods, such as protein, in the that way tissues, such as muscle, can. This is why so many symptoms of altered brain chemistry occur when blood sugar levels drop quickly.

Another point to remember is that when the brain is deprived of glucose, it is also deprived of oxygen. Have you noticed that you yawn when you go too long without food? Poor availability of glucose to the brain can also cause many of the symptoms associated with oxygen deprivation, without blood sugar levels being low. If blood circulation to the head is affected by, say, tension in the neck and shoulders, brain cells are bound to be half-starved, because the blood, which carries the glucose to the brain, is constricted. (You will later see how poor blood circulation to the head can also cause migraine headaches.)

HOW IS BLOOD SUGAR REGULATED?

When food is eaten, the pancreas, an organ on the left side of the body near the stomach, pours out regulated amounts of the hormone called insulin. If this organ is working properly, and if food intake is adequate, then all is well.

WHAT CAN GO WRONG WITH THIS SYSTEM?

Two undesirable things can happen with this system: either the pancreas can be hypoactive and not produce enough insulin, resulting in diabetes, or hyperglycemia; or the pancreas can be hyperactive and produce too much insulin, resulting in low blood sugar, or hypoglycemia.

WHY DOES THE PANCREAS OVERWORK?

The pancreas overworks because it gets the wrong message. When you are in a nervous state, all the nerves in your body are overstimulated. This includes the nerves to the pancreas. So the pancreas is being told: Go faster, go faster. It puts out more and more insulin— much more than the body requires. The result is that the available glucose is quickly used and blood sugar levels drop dramatically.

Common reasons why the pancreas is overstimulated:

- *Extra demands*. Exercise, stress, pregnancy, the premenstrual phase, and the effects of some drugs.

- *Rarer reasons*. Glucose sensitivity, liver disease, disease of the pancreas, and underactivity of the pituitary, thyroid, or adrenal glands.

Why Does a Drop in Blood Sugar Make Me Feel So Awful?

When your brain is starved, it begins to do strange things.

When there are no food stores left, and blood sugar levels are low, the stomach sends a message to the brain saying, "Help! I'm hungry. What are you going to do?" The brain replies, "Don't worry, I'll get you some food (glucose) out of the cupboard (the liver), but in order to unlock the cupboard door, I have to send a messenger with a key." This chemical messenger is a spurt of adrenaline. The good news is that, when the messenger opens the door, glucose will be released and you can keep on going. The bad news is that you have already seen too much of this messenger, because other systems in your body (respiratory and muscular) are not functioning properly as a result of your nerves having been in trouble. Thus the adrenaline induces all the symptoms you dread most: panic, shaking, palpitations, agoraphobia, and so on. Are you beginning to see why it is so important to eat correctly?

SOME PEOPLE ARE RELUCTANT TO CHANGE THEIR EATING HABITS

A client once asked me, "Isn't it stressful to have to keep to a diet when you're already having difficulty coping?" My reply was, "Yes, some people complain, but I point out to them that it is a small price to pay for reduced anxiety and the control of panic attacks." My experience is that people soon feel the benefit of a proper diet and become very enthusiastic. There are also those who become over-confident after a few symptom-free weeks and return to their old eating habits. It usually takes only one panic attack to send them rushing back to the new way of eating.

CAN THE EFFECTS OF DIET LAPSES BE DELAYED?

What you sow one day, you may not reap until the next. It was fascinating to watch a large group of people encounter their symptoms when they strayed from their diet. Panic attacks abounded on Monday mornings. This happened when normal evening meals were replaced by Sunday tea. Large quantities of bread, cakes, and cookies threw blood sugar levels into confusion, resulting in Monday morning panic attacks. Repeated Saturday morning panic attacks usually proved to be alcohol induced. Even a small quantity of alcohol is enough to provoke symptoms if blood sugar levels are unstable. This makes sense, because the main cause of a hangover is hypoglycemia. People are more able to accept the fact that they can precipitate a panic attack by missing a meal than they can accept the fact that eating the wrong foods can do the same thing.

DO I RISK MORE THAN EXHAUSTED NERVES?

Yes, you do. There is a great deal of evidence showing that people who constantly strain their bodies with "kangarooing" blood sugar levels run a greater risk of developing chronic conditions such as diabetes, arthritis, allergies, migraine headaches, asthma, obesity, blackouts, and epilepsy.

WHY DO UNSTABLE BLOOD SUGAR LEVELS UPSET MY DIGESTION?

When insulin is overproduced, it stimulates the stomach, which in turn increases the flow of digestive secretions. This leads to an overly acidic stomach, and can be followed by heartburn, indigestion, food allergies, or hiatus hernia.

WHY DO UNSTABLE BLOOD SUGAR LEVELS TRIGGER MIGRAINE HEADACHES?

Many migraine sufferers associate missed meals with irritability and headaches. As blood sugar levels fall, more blood is pumped to the brain to prevent the levels of glucose from becoming dangerously low. This causes pressure on the cranial nerves. These nerves serve more than the head: that is why migraines also are accompanied by apparently unrelated symptoms. For example, when the nerves to the stomach or liver are involved, symptoms such as diarrhea can occur. If the nerve to the arm is affected, there can be tingling or numbness in the arm or hand.

If increased pressure affects the nerves to the ears, hypersensitivity to sound or tinnitus (ringing in the ears) can result. It is easy to see why visual disturbances, such as difficulty focusing, flashing lights, partial loss of vision, sensitivity to light, and bloodshot eyes, are so often reported by migraine sufferers. Food sensitivities affect blood glucose levels; it follows therefore that they can also trigger migraines.

CAN UNSTABLE BLOOD SUGAR LEVELS CAUSE ACHING JOINTS AND MUSCLES?

When the adrenal glands are exhausted, cortisone production is lowered. A vital function of cortisone, in addition to controlling stress and metabolizing carbohydrates, is to protect the body from inflammation.

This function of cortisone is confirmed by how dramatically arthritic pain can be reduced by treatment with cortisone and other steroids. The fact that rheumatoid arthritis often clears up during pregnancy also confirms this. During pregnancy, the increase in pituitary hormones and cortisone works to counteract the effect of the reduced production of insulin. Therefore, when insulin production is lowered, blood sugar levels do not jump all over the place; they remain stable because pituitary hormone levels and cortisone levels are adequate.

PREMENSTRUAL SYNDROME AND UNSTABLE BLOOD SUGAR LEVELS

More and more pieces of the jigsaw fit together when the part that hormones play in panic attacks is understood. To go back to the overly acid stomach, it does not absorb calcium efficiently. Nerves need calcium to function properly. Reduced levels of calcium lead to hypersensitivity and irritability of the nervous system. The frayed nerves, muscle cramps, and fluid retention of premenstrual syndrome (PMS) can be attributed to lack of calcium and to an imbalance of the sodium and potassium levels. A person feels very uncomfortable when the body is swollen with fluid, but even more uncomfortable when the brain is. Severe headaches, rapid mood swings, and outbursts of rage are distressingly common symptoms of water retention. The premenstrual craving for sweets, chocolates, and other carbohydrates is a sign that all is not well with the blood sugar levels.

WILL I GET DIABETES IF I IGNORE UNSTABLE BLOOD SUGAR LEVELS?

You will not necessarily get diabetes if you ignore unstable blood sugar levels, but you do run the risk of getting diabetes, particularly if you gain a lot of weight, or have a family history of diabetes or other conditions associated with low blood sugar. A pancreas that is working overtime dealing with a refined-carbohydrate diet and long gaps between meals often gives up trying, which leads to diabetes.

OTHER CONDITIONS ASSOCIATED WITH UNSTABLE BLOOD SUGAR LEVELS

Although some physicians do not believe that low blood sugar levels have any connection with the development of chronic disease, others are firmly convinced that sustained unstable blood sugar levels precede many illnesses. They also believe that improvement, and even a cure, can be attained by simply following a proper eating regimen. Here are some of the conditions associated with unstable blood sugar levels: obesity, hyperactivity, anxiety, depression, asthma, loss of interest in sex, fainting, blackouts, facial pain, epilepsy, arthritis, allergies, migraine headaches, stomach ulcers, addictions, and tinnitus. There is no need to be alarmed by this list: eating sensibly prevents unstable blood sugar levels.

Must I Eat Like This Forever?

Don't worry: as your nerves get stronger and your pancreas stops working overtime, you can have treats. You can add all your old favorites to a sensible diet. There is no need to be overly rigid.

What If I'm Overweight?

If you are overweight, the Weight Watcher's diet can help you lose weight as well as stabilize blood sugar levels. The support they offer is also very valuable. Check the Yellow Pages for local numbers.

Case Histories

During the years I ran a tranquilizer-withdrawal support group, several young women and two young men came for help with panic attacks, although they had no drug histories at all. The women had all been trying to lose weight on crash diets or by skipping meals. Both the young men had altered their diets when they took up a regimen of strenuous exercise: one had been eating steak and eggs one day and candy bars the next. When all resumed healthy eating styles, their panic attacks vanished.

John a 34-year-old teacher, had been having migraine headaches since he was in high school. (He had also started smoking in high school.) Smoking inhibited his appetite so much that he skipped breakfast. He was eventually prescribed tranquilizers, because the migraine headaches were attributed to a stressful job. The pills didn't help and he continued to have regular, one-sided, blinding headaches that often resulted in vomiting. As he withdrew from tranquil-izers he ate regular, balanced meals, cut down on his smoking, and never smoked without eating first. He was astonished by how much this regimen helped the headaches.

Suzie was 28 and had suffered from severe PMS for three years. She was depressed and very frightened by the panic attacks and feelings of rage that were part of this syndrome. Her husband was support-ive but they were both very concerned about the effect her behavior was having on their young family. For almost half the month she was bloated and irritable. She was also clumsy: she continually dropped things and could not knit. Her husband noticed that Suzie's hands and face were swollen during the premenstrual phase of her men-strual cycle. He thought that this was because she ate so much choc-olate during this time. Suzie agreed that this was so, and also complained of constipation, a swollen abdomen, and leg cramps during this time of the month. The cramps were so bad that they woke her during the night. After three months on a balanced diet and supplements (see Chapter 10), she lost 14 pounds. She still felt "a little off" premenstrually, but all her other symptoms disappeared.

CHAPTER SEVEN

Digestion

All digestive problems should be investigated by your doctor.

How Poor Digestion Can Lead to Panic Attacks

Poor digestion might not appear to be as important as rapidly changing blood sugar levels or hyperventilation in causing panic attacks. However, it is worth taking a look at why it should be considered: poor digestion can cause a bloated abdomen, which can affect breathing and result in palpitations.

Causes of Poor Digestion

A Nervous Stomach

A nervous stomach can appreciably affect a compromised immune or nervous system, leading you into a vicious circle—the more discomfort there is from eating, the narrower your diet may become. Pleasure from eating may be replaced by anxiety over what can be digested without discomfort, causing you to eliminate more and more foods from your diet, which ultimately leads to poor nutrition. Also, people with digestive problems often look to refined carbohydrates as foods that are easier to digest. However, if your diet lacks protein and roughage it will take quite a lot of refined carbohydrates to satisfy your appetite, resulting in obesity and malnutrition. Or, the opposite may occur: when your appetite is poor, a "Tea and Toast Syndrome" can develop, leading to malnutrition and weight loss.

LACK OF ENZYMES

These are substances that break down the food entering the digestive system. If there is an enzyme deficiency, the small intestine has to cope with food that has not passed through the initial stages of digestion. The result is discomfort from gas and bloating. Taking digestive enzyme supplements or eating a small amount of *well-chewed* raw vegetables before a cooked meal can help alleviate this problem.

TOO MUCH HYDROCHLORIC ACID

Heartburn or an acid stomach indicates you are producing too much hydrochloric acid due to your nervous state. Relieving these symptoms with antacids is fine as a shot-term measure. However, if there is something wrong with the acid/alkaline balance in your stomach it is because you are mistreating your digestive system in some way, such as skipping or rushing meals, not eating enough alkaline-forming foods, or by overstimulating the nerves to the digestive tract.

Water is a good and simple antacid: drink plenty between meals. Vegetable stock is also a good antacid.

GOING TO THE DOCTOR WITH "ACID STOMACH" PROBLEMS   You might be given a simple antacid or a drug in the cimetidine group such as Tagamet. It cannot be denied that these drugs are effective, but it is unwise to stay on them for long periods.

SIDE EFFECTS   I first came across large numbers of people who were given these drugs for gastrointestinal disturbances when they were withdrawing from drugs in the benzodiazepine group (diazepam, or Valium) or lorazepam (Ativan). They were also given to people who were having withdrawal symptoms from antidepressant drugs such as amytriptyline or the MAOI inhibitors.

Many were given cimetidine for long periods without being re-checked. Long after the tranquilizer or antidepressant withdrawal was over, many people reported feeling ill when they tried to stop cimetidine. A rebound overproduction of gastric acid *was* an expect-ed result, but they also reported irritability, insomnia, panic attacks, and a feeling of malaise. On the positive side, many users said that the bowel symptoms (such as constipation and colic, which many had suffered for years) disappeared within two weeks of discontinu-ing the cimetidine or similar drugs.

Tagamet is now available over the counter. It should only be used for a short time and not before you have had a diagnosis from your doctor. If it makes you feel anxious or irritable discontinue using it and look for a natural approach to the problem of overacidity, such as changing your diet and lifestyle. If the symptoms persist, visit your doctor to see if you are producing too little hydrochloric acid.

What to Do

Relaxation and Eating

It goes without saying that if tension and worry are affecting your digestive system, relaxing more will improve matters. In addition, temporarily change the kinds of food you eat. Try the following:

1. Ideally, do two relaxation sessions per day: on waking and before your main meal. If you can't, do ten min-utes of slow breathing (see page 72), before eating.

2. Try changing the room you eat in. Put on some music, set a place with flowers or lovely dishes, being mind-ful of what you are doing when you eat. Try repeating affirmations such as, "I am thankful for this food; it is nourishing every cell in my body." Or, "My digestion is in perfect working order." Even if our conscious mind rejects these affirmations at first, the nerves to your digestive tract will respond as you continue.

3. Chew very slowly. Digestion begins in the mouth where saliva breaks down the starches. If you gulp down your food the first stage of digestion is lost and the stomach has difficulty coping with the nutrients.

4. Increase the amount of protein you eat. If you do not eat meat, poultry, eggs, fish or beans, try high protein drinks (available from most groceries or pharmacies). If you can manage to drink soup, try liquidizing the family meal and add some stock.

5. Buy a juicer for fruit and vegetables.

6. Boil roughly chopped green and root vegetables, add stock powder or cubes. Discard the vegetables and drink the broth water several times a day, hot or cold. This is easily digested and will give you an excellent source of minerals. As your digestion improves you could liquidize some of the vegetables and add them to the stock.

These are natural ways to avoid becoming low in vital nutrients when your digestion is poor. Mineral and vitamin supplements are helpful but many people with poor digestion find them difficult to take.

What Are You Doing to Yourself?

Finally, take a look at what is making you so tense. Can you change your lifestyle, by slowing down, putting yourself first for a while, getting out of destructive relationships, confronting anyone who is demanding too much from you (parents/children, employers), letting go of the past, or changing negative thoughts?

CHAPTER EIGHT

Panic Attacks and Drugs

Any substance that sedates (calms) the nervous system—be it alcohol, prescribed drugs, or street drugs—can be a cause of panic attacks. When adrenaline levels are artificially reduced by drugs, it is like putting a lid on a volcano. When the lid is taken off—through withdrawal—adrenaline rushes out with even greater force. Then all the terrible feelings of panic—palpitations, sweating, and so on—reoccur.

Tranquilizers, Sleeping Pills, and Panic Attacks

Both side effects and withdrawal from tranquilizers and sleeping pills can cause panic attacks. This is confusing and has caused a great deal of distress: the very drugs that are supposed to stop panic attacks can, in some people, actually cause them. It is now well documented that these drugs, known as the benzodiazepines, can produce anxiety at the beginning of treatment. This might occur in a person who hasn't had undue anxiety prior to treatment, perhaps someone who has been prescribed diazepam for muscle spasm. This is called the paradoxical reaction. Withdrawal from these drugs can also cause problems, and must be done slowly and with supervision. During withdrawal, anxiety levels can be six times greater than before the drug was begun, even in people who have been given identical-looking tablets and have no knowledge that their drugs are being withdrawn. It is, therefore, not a matter of, "Uh-oh, I forgot to take my Valium today. I'm going to feel awful." When anxiety rockets sky-high, panic attacks are quite common.

Can Withdrawal Symptoms Appear While I'm Still Taking Tranquilizers or Sleeping Pills?

Withdrawal symptoms may appear while you're taking tranquilizers or sleeping pills, because the body has become dependent on these medications. These symptoms are the body's demand for more medication. You can also have panic attacks between doses. A list of drugs known to cause these symptoms follows, but for full information on the side effects, withdrawal reactions, and a complete withdrawal program, check with your physician.

Chemical name	Brand name
Diazepam	Valium, Valrelease, Zetran
Lorazepam	Ativan, Alzapam
Chlordiazepoxide	Librium, Libritabs, Lipoxide
Temazepam	Restoril
Oxazepam	Serax

Remember, you must *not* stop any prescribed drugs without consulting your doctor. If you come off the drugs slowly and take care of yourself, you can recover completely: countless people have. See the guidelines for professionals on pages 58–59, in case you need information for your doctor.

Can Antidepressants Cause Panic Attacks?

Although it is not widely acknowledged, it is nevertheless true that antidepressants can cause panic attacks. Antidepressants can be very useful drugs, and they dramatically help some people. However, anyone who has worked with large numbers of people on antidepressants cannot fail to observe that at the beginning of therapy the drug can also make the patient feel very anxious. In addition, there is a very well-defined withdrawal syndrome for some people: rebound anxiety or rebound depression can occur when the drug is stopped. This last problem is helped by gradual withdrawal of the medication. Patients are often told that the drug won't help their depression for several weeks; they are rarely told that they could feel more anxious at first, but that the anxiety will pass. This anxiety is one of the main reasons why people discontinue taking the drug after a few days.

The drug Prozac has been in the news lately. For some, it has been a magical relief from depression; for others it has caused unbearable anxiety. Other antidepressant drugs include the following:

> *Amitripytline (Elavil, Endep)*
>
> *Triptaphen*

Do Any Other Prescribed Drugs Cause Panic Attacks?

Drugs that are not prescribed for anxiety, but have a sedative action as a side effect, can also cause panic attacks. These include antihistamines, cimetidine (Tagamet), beta blockers, and, strangely enough, antibiotics. For many years now, people have been reporting psychological symptoms while taking or coming off antibiotics. Most doctors considered these symptoms to be psychosomatic until recently; research now shows that some antibiotics share receptors in the brain with tranquilizers. (A receptor is a specific site on the surface of a cell.)

Cigarettes and Panic Attacks

Nicotine is a pernicious addiction because it both sedates and stimulates. People may smoke cigarettes to calm their nerves, but if they smoke before a meal or smoke too much, they could become very jittery and even experience panic attacks. Panic attacks brought on by cigarette withdrawal have been mentioned in the medical literature. It

(Text continued on page 60.)

Guidelines

(From *Current Problems* [Committee on Safety of Medicines], Number 21, January 1988.)

"Benzodiazepines, Dependence, and Withdrawal Symptoms"

There has been concern for many years regarding benzodiazepine dependence (*British Medical Journal*, 1980, 910–912). Such dependence is becoming increasingly worrying.

Withdrawal symptoms include anxiety, tremor, confusion, insomnia, perception disorders, fits, depression, gastrointestinal, and other somatic symptoms. These may sometimes be difficult to distinguish from the symptoms of the original illness.

It's important to note that withdrawal symptoms can occur with benzodiazepines following therapeutic doses given for short periods of time.

Withdrawal effects usually appear shortly after stopping a benzodiazepine with a short half-life. Symptoms may continue for weeks or months. No epidemiological evidence is available to suggest that one benzodiazepine is more responsible for the development of dependency or withdrawal symptoms than another. The Committee on Safety of Medicines recommends that the use of benzodiazepines should be limited in the following ways.

Uses

AS ANXIOLYTICS

1. Benzodiazepines are indicated for the short-term relief (two to four weeks only) of anxiety that is severe, disabling, or subjecting the individual to unacceptable distress, occurring alone or in association with insomnia or short-term psychosomatic organic or psychotic illness.

2. The use of benzodiazepines to treat short-term "mild" anxiety is inappropriate and unsuitable.

As Hypnotics [Sleep-Inducing Drugs]

3. Benzodiazepines should be used to treat insomnia only when it is severe, disabling, or subjecting the individual to extreme distress.

Dose

1. The lowest dose which can control the symptoms should be used. It should not be continued beyond four weeks.

2. Long-term chronic use is not recommended.

3. Treatment should always be tapered off gradually.

4. Patients who have taken benzodiazepines for a long time may require a longer period during which doses are reduced.

5. When a benzodiazepine is used as a hypnotic, treatment should, if possible, be intermittent.

Precautions

1. Benzodiazepines should not be used alone to treat depression or anxiety associated with depression. Suicide may be precipitated in such patients.

2. They shouldn't be used for phobic or obsessional states.

3. They should not be used for the treatment of chronic psychosis.

4. In case of loss or bereavement, psychological adjustment may be inhibited by benzodiazepines.

5. Disinhibiting effects may be manifested in various ways. Suicide may be precipitated in patients who are depressed, and aggressive behavior towards self and others may be precipitated. Extreme caution should therefore be used in prescribing benzodiazepines in patients with personality disorders.

is worth noting, however, that they may not appear for some months after complete cessation. But don't use this as an excuse for continuing to smoke! The panic attacks are transitory.

Another point worth noting is that if you cut down your smoking by more than one-third at a time, you may experience severe withdrawal symptoms. But having said that, some people don't have any symptoms at all when they stop; others experience only the craving for cigarettes. For those who experience severe physical and emotional symptoms, a word of comfort: this has much more to do with your biochemistry than with your lack of willpower. It is possibly because of these symptoms, and perhaps also a masked allergy factor, that some people find giving up cigarettes to be so difficult. A hidden, or masked, allergy can develop with any substance that is taken into the body daily; when the body is denied the substance, the symptoms appear.

Do You Panic Because You Are Still Smoking?

Some people worry a great deal about being dependent on nicotine, but fail repeatedly in their attempts to stop. These people are often scorned by those who claim that it is only willpower that is required to stop smoking. Willpower certainly plays a significant role in quitting smoking. However, for the physically addicted or allergic smoker, there is a lot more to it: lack of willpower does not cause physical symptoms, some of which are noted in the list that follows.

Some people experience a clearly defined withdrawal syndrome (a collection of symptoms) when they abstain from nicotine. This is not surprising, because the drug affects many systems in the body. Giving up cigarettes is just like giving up heroin, tranquilizers, or any other addictive substance. Common complaints include the following:

— anxiety and depression
— panic attacks
— irritability
— headaches
— confused thoughts

— constipation

— craving for sugar

— craving for coffee

— swollen, aching joints and muscles

— skin problems (small raised red spots seen in detoxification)

People who have tried several times to stop smoking know these feelings very well; they even know which symptoms will come in the first week, how long it takes for joint pains to start, and so on. Unfortunately, they also know how quickly the symptoms go away when they resume smoking.

As you can see, there are a number of reasons why people fail to give up smoking. Lack of information heads the list. If people know what to expect and understand that the symptoms will not last forever, they stand a much better chance of succeeding. Also, if they prepare their bodies for the trauma (make no mistake, smoking cessation can take its toll physically), the chances of success are further improved.

Are You in This Trap?

If you are an addictive smoker, you are likely to have unstable blood sugar levels. Read Chapter 6 carefully and adjust your diet accordingly. If your blood sugar is allowed to drop, you are much more likely to beg someone for a cigarette. Keep a bag of sunflower seeds in your pocket, and eat some every hour between meals at first. Sunflower seeds will keep your blood sugar levels stable. Also, eat foods that leave an alkaline residue, or ash, when they are broken down in the body: vegetables, particularly raw vegetables, and tart fruits are good. Research has shown that an overly acid body is more likely to crave cigarettes.

You Need More Than a Good Diet

Before you stop smoking, take an honest look at your nutritional state, and build your body up so that it can meet the stress of withdrawal. Every cigarette you smoke robs you of 25 mg. of vitamin C, so you are bound to be short of this nutrient.

Requirements for all nutrients rise sharply when your body is under siege. Take a good quality multivitamin and multimineral supplement regularly. If you can identify any particular deficiency, you can take an additional supply of that vitamin or mineral. (It is necessary to understand the interaction of vitamins and minerals to obtain the minimum absorbtion of each. Consult a nutritionist.)

Vitamin C and magnesium both help rid the body of poisons. Vitamin C strengthens the immune system and eases withdrawal symptoms. Vitamin B_3, niacin, has also been found to be helpful in dealing with withdrawal symptoms. This chemical, which can also be bought in the form called nicotinic acid, is similar in structure to nicotine. Niacin is thought to resemble the endogenous benzodiazepine, that is, a tranquilizing substance similar to Valium that is made in the brain. People with certain health conditions, liver disease, stomach ulcers, low blood pressure, gout or hemorrhage should consult with their physician before taking niacin. Don't be surprised if your skin prickles and you look like a beet 20 minutes or so after taking it. This flush is beneficial: it improves circulation to the extremities and acts like an internal sauna. Niacin is also known to be essential to the health of the bowel. In addition, people who are always cold often find this supplement helpful. Many people who take it say that after the first few doses they feel calmer. (To avoid the flush, you could ask for niacinamide, another form of vitamin B_3, but you would lose the benefits of the flush.) Remember to take all the B vitamins if you take niacin. No B vitamin should be taken in isolation, because it would deplete the store of the other B vitamins.

Caffeine and Panic Attacks

So many people drink endless cups of tea and coffee each day and then wonder why they are nervous. A cup of strong tea or coffee on an empty stomach is a potent trigger for a panic attack. Most people don't think of caffeine as a drug, and they also don't realize that it can affect more than the nervous system. Make an effort to cut down on your caffeine intake, particularly if you have sore breasts, allergies, digestive problems, cystitis, or restless legs syndrome (that awful feeling when your legs won't relax and you feel the need to move them even when you are in bed). You might have no trouble at all giving up caffeine completely for a while, or even for good, but it is important to note that some people experience withdrawal symptoms even if they are not heavy tea, coffee, or cola drinkers. Cutting down on caffeine can cause lethargy; total abstinence can result in nausea, severe headache, muscle and joint pains, or depression.

A Blinding Headache

A "caffeine storm" develops when, during withdrawal, all the caffeine that has been stored in the body is released into the bloodstream, causing a form of caffeine poisoning. The resulting headache is particularly severe. (In fact, caffeine addicts are used to test the efficacy of headache drugs.) Typically, as soon as caffeine is ingested, even a small amount, the headache eases. But the same cannot be said for the depression that often accompanies caffeine withdrawal. Some people feel down for several days. Occasionally after complete withdrawal, the depression lasts for months. Homeopathic treatment for caffeine addiction can be helpful in these cases. Check your local health food store for homeopathic remedies. Mild symptoms can often be relieved by putting a grain of coffee or a couple of drops of tea under the tongue.

The preceding information is not meant to discourage you from clearing the caffeine out of your system: your bowels, kidneys, and nervous system would welcome it. I have included this information to help you understand that some of the everyday things we drink are powerful drugs and that some people experience withdrawal symptoms when they stop ingesting them. Cut down slowly if you are one of the unlucky ones. You can do this by mixing decaffeinated coffee or tea with your usual blend and then increasing the ratio of decaffeinated to caffeinated drink until you are drinking a decaffeinated brew. Also, choose a brand that does not use chemicals in the decaffeination process.

Street Drugs and Panic Attacks

All the illegal drugs can cause panic attacks. Those who take LSD, speed (amphetamines), or cocaine, as well as those who mix street drugs and benzodiazepines (tranquilizers and sleeping pills), are most at risk. Many people who use marijuana see it as an innocuous substance. As I see it, this is far from the truth. As with any drug, marijuana can cause serious psychological problems, including a nervous breakdown, and it is common for regular users to suffer panic attacks and depression during withdrawal.

Jet Lag and Panic Attacks

The relationship between jet lag and panic attacks has nothing to do with the fear of flying. Attacks occur after the journey, usually for about a week. Typically they take the form of mild panic attacks on waking, but they can also occur at other times during the day. They may be a result of blood sugar levels being disturbed by eating against the body clock, or they may be due to increased levels of the brain chemical serotonin.

The latter results in the serotonin irritation syndrome. The air around us is charged with negative and positive ions. When there is an excess of positive ions, animals have been shown to become restless, irritable, and anxious. It affects sensitive humans as well, usually weather-sensitive people. Have you ever felt swollen, too tight for your skin, or headachy with a stuffy nose before a storm, or when there was a warm wind, or during a full moon? You might also feel anxious or depressed: "under the weather." When positive ions and your anxiety levels are both high, it might take only a small trigger to bring on a panic attack. A small machine that produces negative ions (an ionizer) is the answer to this problem. These are available in most department stores. (They are also very helpful for people with allergies or chest problems.) Negative ions are also produced by running water (even a shower). They are also found by the ocean. For further information, read *The Ion Effect* by Fred Soyka (Bantam, 1978).

PART TWO
Helping Yourself

CHAPTER NINE

Improve Your Breathing

Choose to Live: B-R-E-A-T-H-E

Life is breath. It is the most important function of the body. We may be able to fast and go without fluids for a while, but we cannot stop breathing for more than a few minutes. So it must be the most important bodily function we have. Correct breathing has a profound effect on your nervous system, thought processes, and even spiritual life. Careless breathing shortens your lifespan and predisposes you to a great many diseases, not only diseases of the respiratory system, but of every system of the body.

Why Have We Developed Poor Breathing Habits?

Human beings in industrialized societies have developed tense attitudes in walking, sitting, and standing: the shoulders are raised, the chest is narrowed, and the head is pulled back. This posture does not allow us to use our full lung capacity. Animals, children, and people in nonindustrialized societies do not have this problem.

The Holding Breath

Do you hold your breath? Psychoanalyst Wilhelm Reich noticed that many of his patients held their breath and delayed breathing out in order to control their feelings. This serves to slow down the metabolic rate (the rate at which calories are burned), which reduces the flow of adrenaline and thus temporarily alleviates anxiety.

Control Your Breath, Control Your Life

The amount of energy you have is in proportion to the way you breathe. When you inhale you are taking in more than the components of air: you are also taking in the life force (also called *prana*, the vital force, universal energy, or chi). You will not find reference to the life force in *Gray's Anatomy*, but that does not mean it does not exist. In Western thought, we are just beginning to see what our Eastern brothers and sisters have been aware of for thousands of years. However, acceptance is slow because of a lack of "evidence": life force doesn't leave a chemical residue, and it's difficult to measure this energy in conventional terms. We have a lot to learn. But the life force is there for the taking. Are you using it?

How Is This Energy Used?

Prana is taken in by the nervous system and gives us strength and vitality. This energy is used, and must be replenished in the same way as oxygen and food. If the supply of *prana* is not enough, you become devitalized. We speak of the sufferer as having low energy, having run-down batteries, or being drained. In order to have a healthy body, the supply of *prana* has to be adequate, and must have free access to all parts of the body.

WHAT CAUSES BLOCKAGES IN THE FLOW OF PRANA?

Poor breathing, tension, injury, bad posture, disease, worry, and sending negative thought patterns to parts of the body all cause blocks in the flow of *prana*. If you become "blocked," you can help yourself by using breathing exercises, stretching exercises, meditation, relaxation, or yoga. Also, most recognized alternative therapies increase the supply and regulate the flow of *prana*. These therapies include acupuncture, acupressure, shiatsu, yoga, t'ai chi, massage, homeopathy, aromatherapy, reflexology, and therapeutic touch.

Start Breathing Properly Today

Controlled breathing can put you in charge of every aspect of your life. It not only improves your physical health, but also helps you to master fear and other unwanted emotions, such as anger and jealousy. Learning the science of breath is one of the most important ways that you can improve your life.

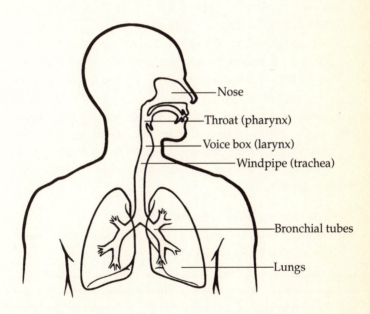

Nose

Throat (pharynx)

Voice box (larynx)

Windpipe (trachea)

Bronchial tubes

Lungs

What Do We Breathe With?

We breathe with the lungs (two spongy sacs) and the air passages leading to them. The air passages are the nose, the throat (pharynx), the voice box (larynx), the windpipe (trachea), and the bronchial tubes. Together these make up the respiratory system (see illustration above).

SOME QUESTIONS ABOUT BREATHING

- *Mouth or nose breathing?*
When you breathe through the nose, the air is warmed and germs and other impurities are filtered out. When you breathe through the mouth, this does not happen. The result is a parched tongue, dry throat, and often a cough. You must have noticed these symptoms when you have had a blocked nose.

- *How does the air get into the lungs?*
The strong, sheetlike muscle called the diaphragm, which separates the chest from the abdomen, draws air into the lungs.

- *Can I control the action of this muscle?*
Although the action of the diaphragm is automatic (like the action of the heart) *it can come under the control of the will.* This is the first thing you need to know when you start to retrain your breathing. Although this muscle functions automatically, if you give it lazy messages and imprison it with tension, it can become very lax. When the diaphragm expands, the capacity of the lungs is increased and air rushes in; when it relaxes, the air is pushed out.

- *How does poor breathing affect circulation?*
Blood pumped by the heart is transported via the arteries to tiny tubes called capillaries. The blood reaches and nourishes every part of the body. It is bright red and full of vital nutrients. When it returns via the veins to the heart, dull and poisoned by the waste products of metabolism, it then goes to the lungs, where a clean-up operation begins. The success of that operation depends on *how* you breathe.

- *Do you have dirty blood?*
Good breathing assures that "clean" blood will be poured back into the system. Poor breathing will result

in "dirty" blood being returned to the system. Poor breathing is rather like using the same dirty bathwater over and over again. Would you do that to your skin?

- *When you have clean blood*
  When blood is properly exposed to the air in the lungs, it is not only cleaned, it also takes up the oxygen needed to nourish the whole body. This is essential for all systems, especially the digestive system, to function properly. Poor digestion and hyperventilation often go hand in hand. Insufficient oxygen means poor absorption of food, poor elimination of waste, and chronic malaise.

Types of Breathing

- *Shoulder breathing (hyperventilation)*
  This is the worst type of breathing; it is nothing less than dangerous. Air fills only the upper portion of the lungs, so the cells do not receive enough oxygen to work properly.

- *Rib breathing*
  This is marginally better, but not good enough. Air fills the middle of the lungs and covers a larger area.

- *Abdominal and diaphragmatic breathing*
  This is a great improvement: the ribs and the muscles of the abdomen are relaxed, allowing the lungs to expand fully and breathe in more air.

- *The complete or full breath*
  This is an excellent way to breathe. Air fills all three partitions of the lungs. There is plenty of movement in the whole chest. All the air cells and breathing muscles, including the muscles between the ribs, are used. When the diaphragm expands and the ribs are pushed out, the lungs have room to inflate. If you don't move these muscles, it's like trying to inflate a balloon inside a small box.

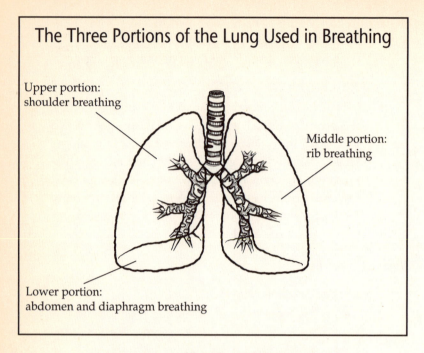

The Three Portions of the Lung Used in Breathing

Upper portion:
shoulder breathing

Middle portion:
rib breathing

Lower portion:
abdomen and diaphragm breathing

Treat Yourself: Take a Full Breath

Imagine that your chest has three sections and each one is a colored balloon:

    1. The shoulder balloon is blue.

    2. The rib balloon is green.

    3. The abdomen and diaphragm balloon is yellow.

BECOMING AWARE OF THE THREE SECTIONS

    1. Stand or sit with a straight back, and breathe into the blue balloon; lift your shoulders toward your ears and breathe in. Notice what it feels like to inflate the top part of your lungs.

(Relax)

    2. In the same position, push out the chest and ribs and breathe into the green balloon. Be aware of how different that feels.

(Relax)

   3. Breathe into the yellow balloon by pushing the front wall of your abdomen, above your navel, slightly down and out, and notice how much space you are making inside. You will feel the tension in your gut release as you do this.

(Relax)

Imagine the balloons are in boxes and that when you use your muscles you are opening the boxes to allow the balloons to fill with air. A complete breath is impossible if the balloons are imprisoned.

By now you should be aware of these three distinct "boxes." Bringing the breath into all three boxes in a flowing, rhythmic movement is the secret of the complete breath. The movements are not jerky or vigorous, but rather slow and peaceful.

Be patient when you practice controlled breathing: it is not easy. Work for at least two 15-minute sessions per day. You will find that the results are well worth it. If you like, you can build these exercises into your daily activities. Practice them while you wait for the pot to boil, when you're in line for the restroom, or when you take a short stroll at lunchtime. At this stage, there is no need to count how many breaths you take per minute: your breathing will naturally be slowed. It takes much longer to use the shoulders, ribs, abdomen, and diaphragm to breathe.

As you breathe in:

- slightly lift the shoulders,
- expand the chest and ribs, and
- lift the abdomen and diaphragm.

As you breathe out:

- let the shoulders fall,
- let the ribs sink back, and
- pull the abdomen and diaphragm in and then gently up to push out the last of the air.

Are Some People Afraid to Change Their Breathing?

You may be nervous about changing your breathing habits. Perhaps this is because when you have tried this, you have felt lightheaded or breathless. This happens because you have changed the levels of carbon dioxide in your blood too quickly, bringing on the very symptoms you fear. This illustrates just how unhealthy your breathing is. You need to have a rest and start again, going at the right speed for you. You also need to know that if you persevere, the lightheadedness will disappear and a feeling of relaxation will take over. If you have been breathing rapidly from the upper chest it is unrealistic to try to breathe eight times a minute during your first attempt at controlled breathing. Change the rate and depth of your breathing in stages. It might be better to master abdominal and diaphragmatic breathing first: it is not quite as good as complete breathing, but it is still very helpful. Abdominal and diaphragmatic breathing also requires less concentration, so it can be done while you are walking around or working.

Become Aware of How You Are Breathing

It will take time for better breathing habits to become automatic, so be patient with yourself. To see how many times per minute you are breathing, look at a watch or clock after you have been at rest for a few minutes. Count how many times you breathe in and out (this is one breath) in 30 seconds; double this and you have your respiration rate per minute. If it is 16 or more breaths, you would be wise to practice the exercise that follows. If you find it difficult to count your breaths, ask a family member to do it for you when you are unaware of what he or she is doing.

EXERCISE

You might find this exercise boring, but the results will be rewarding. Some people have difficulty raising the abdomen. It helps to place a warm, covered, hot water bottle on the stomach: it relaxes you and also gives you a little weight to lift. Some people find lying on the stomach easier: the resistance of the floor or bed is helpful.

1. Place one hand on the stomach and one on the chest. The hand on the chest should stay as still as possible. The hand on the stomach will go up and down as you breathe.

2. Breathe out through the nose (don't force it), and let the stomach fall gently as you do so.

3. Breathe in through the nose, letting the stomach rise. Try to make the "out" breath longer than the "in" breath.

4. Gradually train yourself to breathe between eight and twelve times per minute.

The aim is to breathe slowly, lifting the abdomen. If you breathe deeply, you may become lightheaded or your heart may skip a little. This shows you how it is not only low carbon dioxide levels but also rapid changes in the levels of carbon dioxide that can cause symptoms. This is nothing to worry about: if you get anxious, take a rest and start again.

Am I Getting It Right?

People are often anxious about breathing correctly. Your body will tell you whether you are getting it right. You will begin to feel calmer, there might be a few gurglings in your stomach (this is tension being released from the bowels), or you might feel muscles letting go of tension. Remember, it takes time to achieve this: it does not happen in the first couple of minutes.

Using Breathing to Cope with Panic Attacks

If your attitude is, I will die (be sick, faint, wet myself) if I don't fight this panic attack, you will encourage more attacks. Your attitude will be a trigger for further attacks: the adrenaline levels will shoot up and it will start all over again. You can train yourself to break this vicious circle. If you are going into a situation that you know has caused you to panic before, stop and visualize breathing slowly and coping well with the situation before you go. Teach yourself to link the words *slow breathing* with the word *panic*. Write the words down together over and over again.

First Aid for Panic Attacks: Bag Rebreathing, Cold Water, and Sweet Food or Drink

Make an effort to increase your levels of carbon dioxide. Holding a paper (never plastic) bag around your nose and mouth, cup your hands around your nose and mouth, and breathe normally. Do not puff or blow into the bag: you will make your symptoms worse. As you breathe in your own carbon dioxide from the bag, you will feel better.

You can also use bag rebreathing to prevent symptoms. Some people use bag rebreathing routinely during the day to prevent panic attacks. To leave your hands free, poke two holes in the upper edge of a bag (one on each side), strengthen the holes with adhesive tape or gummed rings to prevent tearing, and then thread elastic through the holes. (This resembles a horse's nose bag.) Some people find that oxygen masks work well; others use the masks used by painters or people working with dust. The latter can also be used as a convenient frame for a paper bag: cut out the middle of the mask and attach the bag around the edges with adhesive tape. You can buy these masks at pharmacies or hardware stores.

Cold water also helps some people prevent panic attacks. You can splash your face with cold water or put something cold, such as a bag of frozen peas or an ice pack, over your nose and cheeks. Some people find this helps to slow down their breathing.

As soon as you feel steadier, you must eat or drink something sweet. However, this is only a temporary measure, as you will see in the next chapter.

CHAPTER TEN

A Healthy Diet

Eating to Keep Blood Sugar Levels Stable

It is impossible to create a diet plan that suits everyone. As long as you stick to the principles of the following plans, the choices are yours. You might be a vegetarian, in which case you will need to add lots of nuts and whole grains to your diet; you might be on a macrobiotic diet; you might already have a good diet but poorly space your meals; or you might be a junk-food diner about to reform. (If you are a vegetarian or on a macrobiotic diet, check to make certain you don't have a vitamin B_{12} deficiency. Please note that if your doctor has already given you a diet to follow, you should consult him or her *before you make any changes in your eating pattern.*)

Principles of the Diet

Don't go longer than two-and-one-half to three hours without eating. Snack between meals on healthy foods, eat a snack as late as possible before bed, and, in order to minimize rapid changes of the level of glucose in the blood, always avoid foods and substances that are absorbed into the bloodstream quickly.

Avoid, or Cut Down to a Minimum, Refined Carbohydrates

Sugar, candy, chocolate, white bread, white flour, cakes, cookies, pastries, alcohol, sweet drinks, and junk foods are all refined carbohydrates.

Eat Complex (unrefined) Carbohydrates

Whole grain cereals, wheat, oats, barley, rice, rye, and millet are examples of complex carbohydrates. Give up processed breakfast cereals, and make your own muesli from whole oats, nuts, seeds (sunflower, pumpkin, or sesame are all very nutritious), and a few raisins, sultanas, or dried apricots. Make sure your brown bread is whole grain. Whole grain cookies, sweetened with apple juice, a small amount of fructose, or dried fruit, are a special treat.

Eat Protein

This is going to be a trial-and-error process. Some people feel well and energetic when they eat more protein. It helps to rid the body of excess water. Others find that it does not suit them, and they prefer to concentrate on complex carbohydrates. Overweight people do well on the Weight Watcher's diet, which includes protein in every meal.

> *Animal proteins:* Meat, fish, poultry, cheese, eggs, milk, and yogurt
>
> *Vegetable proteins:* Nuts, seeds, peas, beans, and lentils

Eat Large Quantities of Vegetables

Vegetables will supply you with essential minerals and vitamins as well as provide roughage. Some people have become overly anxious about roughage, eating bran with everything. This is not a good idea: bran can irritate the bowel and hinder the absorption of some minerals. Eating vegetables is a better way to get roughage.

EAT LOTS OF FRESH FRUIT

Apples are said to be particularly good: the pectin acts as a blood sugar stabilizer. Although fruit contains quite a lot of sugar, it is in a form (fructose) that does not need insulin for its digestion. Fresh fruit is an ideal food that helps to slow down the pancreas.

EAT SOME FAT

People tend to concentrate on low-fat diets and think that this will take care of all their cholesterol problems. Yes, by all means, cut down on animal fat, but remember that there are other factors that are just as important as cholesterol: stress and a diet low in vegetables and fruit can be just as damaging as moderate amounts of butter. Also, remember that some foods actually lower cholesterol levels. These include onions, garlic, apples, and olive oil. (Olive oil is also wonderful for the immune system, which is the body's defense against disease.)

A Suggested Diet

AS SOON AS YOU GET UP, OR WHILE YOU'RE STILL IN BED: A small glass of unsweetened juice or a piece of fruit.

BREAKFAST: More fruit juice and

—either—

Grilled bacon, fish, eggs, baked beans, cold ham, cheese, or any protein dish, plus mushrooms or tomatoes. One slice of whole grain bread, two crispbreads, rice cakes, and so on, with butter or margarine.

—or—

Oatmeal sweetened with a few raisins, or muesli made from whole oats, nuts, seeds (sunflower, pumpkin, or sesame), and a little dried fruit, or plain yogurt with fresh fruit and nuts, fruit yogurt, or cottage cheese. Bread as already discussed.

Weak tea with milk, if desired, or one cup of weak coffee.

SNACK (TWO HOURS AFTER BREAKFAST): Fruit, yogurt, milk, seeds, nuts, or cheese and crackers.

LUNCH: Any protein dish, hot or cold: meat, fish, chicken, cheese, eggs, sardines, tuna, and so on, or any bean, lentil, or nut dish.

Lots of salad or vegetables, one slice of whole grain bread, or two crispbreads.

SNACK (TWO-AND-ONE-HALF TO THREE HOURS AFTER LUNCH): Weak tea or milk and crispbread with cheese or fruit-only jam; or the same as the midmorning snack.

SNACK (HALF AN HOUR BEFORE DINNER): A small glass of fruit juice.

DINNER: Same as lunch, plus fruit.

SUPPER: Crispbreads, butter, cheese, pâté, and so on. A milk drink, weak tea, or herb tea.

This might look like a lot of food, but remember that there is no need to eat large quantities. Small and often is the rule.

RULES

- Don't skip meals.
- Eat regularly.
- Avoid white flour and sugary foods and drinks; cut out (or at least cut down on) caffeine, cigarettes (if you must smoke, make sure that you have eaten), and alcohol.
- Always have protein in your breakfast.
- Never eat a starch-only meal (bread, cake, or cereal).

Other Suggestions for Blood Sugar Problems

WILL ANY SUPPLEMENTS HELP THE BLOOD SUGAR PROBLEM?

Most health food stores carry an inexpensive supplement called glucose tolerance factor (GTF), which contains chromium.

Many symptoms of PMS are also symptoms of low blood sugar. Chromium is also helpful for PMS sufferers, who are often also short of vitamin B_3, niacinamide. In the premenstrual phase, 100 mg. daily of B_6, and, for the rest of the month, 50 mg. daily, helps reduce water retention and clumsiness. Calcium helps eliminate leg cramps.

Potassium and B$_6$ both help distended abdomens, but because these are stimulants, it is better to take them in the morning. Magnesium can reduce constipation; it is also thought to make the pancreas less sensitive to glucose, thereby slowing down the production of insulin. Magnesium can stop PMS food cravings. A dose of around 300 mg. of magnesium daily for six weeks can be helpful. Evening primrose oil is also very helpful for PMS, although it might be a couple of months before you feel its benefit.

FOOD SENSITIVITIES AND UNSTABLE BLOOD SUGAR LEVELS

Food sensitivities can cause blood sugar levels to fluctuate. Symptoms include heart palpitations, flushes, bloating, restlessness, insomnia, mood changes, and a stuffy nose after eating certain foods. The foods that most often cause allergies are wheat, milk, beef, citrus fruits, sugar, and coffee. Any food, however, can cause allergies.

Before embarking on drastic exclusion diets that can cause dramatic weight loss, severely affecting the immune and nervous systems, simply try eliminating junk food and eating a well-balanced diet.

Cleansing the colon can also be very helpful. If the bowel is inflamed you might have to be gentle with your cleansing program. The amino acid L-Glutamine and aloe vera juice are soothing and healing substances for the bowel. Some people do very well on a bulking agent such as Metamucil or slippery elm powder (not the drink, which includes milk) from the health food store.

FIRST AID FOR UNSTABLE BLOOD SUGAR SYMPTOMS

If you find yourself in trouble and there is nothing else to eat but a chocolate bar—say you are driving on the highway—choose one with nuts in it if possible. Remember to eat a nutritious snack as soon as possible. The benefits of a chocolate bar will last only about an hour.

If you are out and feel a panic attack coming on, a cup of coffee or tea with sugar, or a chocolate bar, should be regarded as an emergency measure only.

MACROBIOTIC DIET

If you have the discipline to follow this clean, healthy way of eating, which relies mainly on brown rice and vegetables, you will find

Mishio Kushi's book on blood sugar levels, *Diabetes and Hypogly-caemia: A Natural Approach* (Japan Publications, 1985) very interesting.

Withdrawal From Alcohol or Drugs and Blood Sugar Levels

It is often difficult to separate the symptoms of withdrawal from those of low blood sugar. After all, a large part of a hangover is due to hypoglycemia. It is, therefore, essential to be extremely vigilant about your diet if you are in withdrawal from alcohol, street drugs, or prescribed drugs (tranquilizers, sleeping pills, antidepressants, or hormone replacement therapy). You stand a much better chance of completing withdrawal and of avoiding panic attacks if you eat a proper diet.

Don't Try to Conform to Other People's Eating Habits

If possible, explain to those close to you that you need to keep a steady supply of glucose to the brain to help your nervous system. You are important: ignore any *Are you eating again?* looks. Carry snack foods, such as nuts, fruit, or crispbread, with you at all times.

Fashions come and go with regard to which diet is best suited to control the symptoms of unstable blood glucose levels. (It is now accepted that diet can also help the corresponding rise in cortisol levels.) I have always favored diets such as *The Zone* by Barry Sears that are fairly high in protein. Recent research by Dr. Elias Ilyia has found that a ration of one part protein to seven parts carbohydrate is the most effective eating plan for controlling blood glucose levels.

If You Are Not Convinced That Diet Is Important, Read On

Even after painstaking counseling, some people are reluctant to accept that their eating style makes their symptoms worse. Some even get annoyed at the suggestion that their dramatic symptoms could be helped by diet. My advice is usually to ask them to write down what they eat and when they eat, and also to write down when their panic attacks occur. This method never fails to convince doubters. Try it!

CHAPTER ELEVEN

Conquering Chronic Muscle Spasm

Release makes the energy necessary for change

—Sigmund Freud

Tight Muscles and Panic Attacks

Some people are unwilling to accept that there is a connection between panic attacks and muscle tension. And they are very resistant to the idea that they are going to have to move in order to get better. By the end of this chapter, I hope you will understand the havoc it causes in your nervous system when you walk in a tense manner, sit with your shoulders around your ears, or sleep with your jaw clenched and knees drawn up. Panic attacks can serve as a warning to take a look at what is going on in your emotional life.

What Causes Chronic Muscle Tension?

Chronic muscle tension can be caused by a continual state of fear, even if the fear is not acknowledged or not. The body does not lie.

Imagine a cat stretched out in front of the fire, his muscles relaxed and at their full length. Now imagine that a strange dog walks in: the cat jumps to his feet and arches his back, ready to spring. You must have seen the cartoon cat Tom (of Tom and Jerry) in this attitude many times: back arched, head forward, and paws all bunched together. His muscles are contracted because he's afraid. Many of us walk around in a similar contracted state. Clients often react with astonishment when I take them to a mirror to show them how they are holding their heads and necks. They have no idea that their shoulders are around their ears and their heads are pulled back.

What Effect Does Chronic Muscle Tension Have?

Tension or muscle spasm causes muscles to contract so that they cannot, even at rest, return to their original length and shape. Circulation to the muscles is then affected. Because the lymphatic drainage is also affected, toxins that are left after the muscles have been nourished cannot be swept away and excreted. These toxins form crystals and cause pain, stiffness, and sometimes inflammation and swelling. Muscles in this state are like a shirt that has been repeatedly washed in detergent but not rinsed out. Chronic muscular tension produces not only local muscle pain, but also pulls joints out of alignment, causing more pain. This pain has a profound effect on the mind and can cause anxiety, panic, self-dissatisfaction, or depression.

Where Does This Tension Come From?

Chronic muscular tension can be the effect of present stress or a reflection of past unhappiness, such as rejection, deprivation, frustration, or suppression of anger. We sometimes put our pain in the joints and muscles of our bodies. Tension is sometimes called *armoring*, because it restricts movement, stops us from displaying our feelings, and offers some protection from the hurts of life. Armor is the outer edge of neurosis.

What Happens If I Keep the Armor On?

Apart from pain, tension can have other physical consequences, such as disturbing digestion or making the immune system less efficient. More important, armoring prevents you from getting back to the real you, the person you were when you came into the world, the one you were before you donned the suit of armor to protect your vulnerability. The one you were before you were taught to bend your thoughts and feelings to be acceptable or to meet the expectations of those around you. The one you were before you used the psychological ploys of rationalization, denial, or projection—before you shed what has been called your first nature. Now that you are saddled with your second nature, how do you get back to where you started? Tension becomes so ingrained in your second nature that you don't notice it.

Using Emotional Pain for Growth

Personal crisis—even a nervous breakdown—can be a good opportunity to go down, to touch bottom (you can't go any further than that), and to gain a firm foothold to use in order to come back up to emotional health. Look at your pain, accept it, and start rebuilding your life.

What Is Emotional Health?

To be emotionally healthy, you need to be able to fully experience your feelings without using overbreathing, holding the breath, the armor of chronic muscular tension, drugs, continual activity, or dysfunctional relationships to stand between you and your feelings. Emotional health means being real, not living in denial. To be real means to be aware of your own feelings and needs and to make them of primary importance. To not live in denial means to not deny your own feelings and needs, to not be what others expect you to be out of a fear of not being loved or liked.

Taking the Armor Off

Full breathing and the relaxation of chronic muscular tension releases the energy that is used to maintain the armoring. Growth is not possible without giving up the armor of tension. Try the following:

- *Surrender to your body*
  What will happen if I relax, I let go? Will I lose control? Will I fall? Some people are afraid to relax, because often this is when they take a deep breath—and they overbreathe. This overbreathing causes a surge of adrenaline and panic. (Many people also report panic when they sit down to watch television, because this is when they relax.)

- *Open your body*
  Until you open your body by releasing tension, until you choose to live, you cannot fully know yourself. Self-realization is impossible without knowing the needs of your inner child, the real you. These needs are hidden from you. The constant battle to contain your neurosis has been your way of coping with your feelings and needs, but this battle has also made you anxious and dispirited. You can't keep up this charade any longer.

- *Breathe, let the muscles go, give in*
  Shout, cry, scream if necessary (read *The Primal Scream* by Arthur Janov, Ph.D.). Grounded, integrated people are comfortable with their bodies, with their real selves (their inner child); their center is peaceful. They are not crying inside.

Your Body Has Needs

On a cramped 17-hour flight I was on, a video invited passengers to do ten minutes of simple airplane aerobics. This involved stretching your arms up, rotating your hands and feet, and so on. An embarrassed silence took over, and I was interested to see how many people participated: only six (all women) as far as I could see. People are often unwilling to acknowledge that their bodies have needs.

Releasing the Tension

Good health depends not only on taking in energy—in the form of food, oxygen, and *prana* but also on discharging excess energy. It is common for anxious people and migraine sufferers to say, "I feel as though my body is full of electricity. I feel all charged up. I feel as though I'm having tiny electric shocks all over my body. I feel as though I'm going to burst." These people are not discharging their excess energy. Such people often have extremely tense feet. The feet often hurt, particularly under the instep. The arches are raised: such people are not grounding themselves.

Grounding

Bringing energy into the legs and feet stops you from being "all in your head." It gives you a good base; it stabilizes you. Releasing your feet provides a safety valve for the discharge of pent-up energy, and as the tension dissipates, fear, anger, and hurt can be expressed. It is only by discharging our overloaded circuits that we can avoid blowing a fuse, exploding—or burnout.

Working with the Feet

Reflexology (a type of foot massage that is very relaxing and beneficial to the whole body) is wonderful for tense feet, but if you cannot afford this treatment, there is a great deal you can do for yourself:

- *Foot massage*
  It's a great help to massage your feet twice daily, using any oil or moisturizer you have. Spend at least five minutes on each foot, and finish with gentle stroking toward your knees. To pamper yourself, use aromatherapy oil. Either use the oil for massage, or, to really

relax, massage your feet first, and follow this with a footbath with a few drops of the oil in the water. (Aromatherapy essential oils are potent medicine and should be treated as such.) Inhalation of the sedative oils is very calming, because they work on the part of the brain called the limbic system. Incidentally, this is the part of the brain where tranquilizers work. Aromatherapy books give you complete instructions on choosing and mixing oils. You can also use alternate hot and cold footbaths: two minutes in each for ten minutes. End your foot bath with cold water.

- *Walking barefoot*
  Whenever you can, walk barefoot on grass with your big toes pointing upward. This brings your tense arch in contact with the ground. People who get electric shocks when they touch the refrigerator, or when they are in stores, find this very helpful. Walking on the shore, particularly on ridged sand, is also beneficial. Walking in the water is even better: it is very soothing for the entire nervous system.

- *Releasing leg tension*
  Fear often prevents energy from entering the legs. Many people lock their knees, fearing that they will fall over if they don't. Bringing energy through the legs feels threatening to some people. It suggests descent, going down into the unknown: perhaps the soul, or sadness. A physical descent can also induce fear: being lowered to the ground, going down steps, going down in an elevator, or landing in an airplane. This might be connected to the instinctive fear of falling. To free your legs, lie on a bed and kick vigorously until you are tired, or lie on your back in the swimming pool and kick as hard as you can. (You can hold the bar behind you if you are a nonswimmer.)

Bioenergetic Exercises

Bioenergetic exercise is an alternative therapy that uses the language of the body to heal the problems of the mind. A full description is found in *Bioenergetics* by Alexander Lowen, Ph.D.

EXERCISE ONE

1. Hold onto a chair for support, and stand on one leg with your knee slightly bent. Your leg may tremble: the trembling is tension being released. Hold this position until the discomfort gets to be too much, and then fall forward onto cushions or a blanket.

2. Repeat with the other leg.

3. Do the exercise a second time.

EXERCISE TWO

Bend forward with your knees slightly bent, and touch the ground with your fingertips. Try to hold this position until your legs have had a good shake. Rest and repeat.

Tension in the Jaw

Forget all you have been told about keeping your chin up or a stiff upper lip. This is just a way to stop you from crying, and what's wrong with crying? If pollen gets up your nose, you sneeze. Pain hurts: why not cry? A tense jaw won't allow it. You need to drop your chin before you can give in to some good, therapeutic sobs. Think of how a baby's lower lip quivers and drops just before she cries. People with compressed lips are said to be tightlipped. This posture can serve to hold in what you really want to say, or guard against "swallowing" what other people are saying. A set jaw is thought to be a sign of strength, but actually it can be very uncomfortable. To relax it, pretend to yawn: this makes air rush into the lungs and also helps to release the tension. To prevent your jaw from tightening up again, place your tongue just behind your front teeth.

Crying

Are you able to cry only when you are pushed hard and then become angry with the person who pushed you, or if you are angry with yourself? Does crying feel like failure? Does it feel like weakness?

You might say, "No, I am always crying." But what about the quality of that crying? Is it just overflow that you are discharging? There will be no real release until the energy that is crushing your feelings comes away in sobs that rock your being, sobs that come from way down in your solar plexus: noisy and uncontrolled.

Until you can commit yourself to working with your body, to opening the cage and releasing your imprisoned emotions, you cannot expect to be either physically or psychologically well.

Tension in the Scalp

Hold your head, with your fingers meeting at the midline. Move the scalp from side to side. Massage the temples, brow, behind the ears, and the base of the skull. Then massage all over the head, as though you were washing your hair. Open your eyes wide in an expression of fear and then relax.

Tension in the Shoulders

When your shoulders and brow are raised, and your head is pushed forward, you are displaying a fearful attitude. Around the base of the skull, where the head and neck join, the muscles can be very sore. Where the neck joins the shoulders, the tensing of the anterior, middle, and posterior scalene muscles creates the effect of a rope around the neck. The tightening of these muscles cramps the upper ribs and affects breathing by constricting the opening to the chest. (It can also affect the voice.)

TO RELEASE THE SHOULDERS:

1. Breathe in slowly, raising your shoulders; let them drop as you breathe out.

2. Let your arms hang limply by your sides. Imagine that there is a piece of chalk on the tip of each shoulder, and draw clockwise circles with your shoulders.

3. Standing up, do "windmills" with your arms.

If you can get to a pool, it will be helpful to do these exercises in the water.

Head, Neck, and Shoulder Massage

If you can find a friend to give you the simple massage that follows, you will find great benefit. Some people don't attempt massage, because they feel only trained people can do it. This is not so: anyone can bring relief to tight muscles. There are, however, a few don'ts.

- Don't massage over broken skin, varicose veins, inflamed skin, the heart, the stomach, or the front of the neck, or if there is a malignant disease.

- Don't get tense as you work. If you breathe slowly and relax, you will be much more effective.

INSTRUCTIONS FOR THE HELPER

When you have done this massage a few times, you will be able to feel the tense muscles: they feel gluey, or harder, and resist the pressure of your fingers. Just work away in these areas, and you will feel the muscles becoming less taut. Your fingers are bringing more blood to the area while allowing waste products to be taken away.

Don't be overly concerned about technique. If your thoughts are gentle toward your partner, and you desire to help her, you can't do any harm. Just follow the rules in the preceding section, and let your fingers take over. The following guidelines will assist you:

Sitting down, be as relaxed as you can be; let your breath out as you drop your shoulders; balance your partner's head; make sure her back is straight, but slack; and press her shoulders gently down.

1. Take the energy down to the feet by massaging under the instep in a circular motion, and then give both feet

a brisk rub. If the person can't bear to have her feet massaged, hold them with the backs of your hands together, and with the fingers under the arch of the foot, press into the instep.

2. Stand behind your partner, hold her head in both hands with your fingers meeting at the top, and move the scalp from side to side. Then move your fingers all over the scalp, as if you were washing her hair.

3. Support her forehead with your left hand if you are righthanded. (Use the opposite hand if you are left-handed.) Ask your partner to "give" you her head: to drop her head forward into your hand.

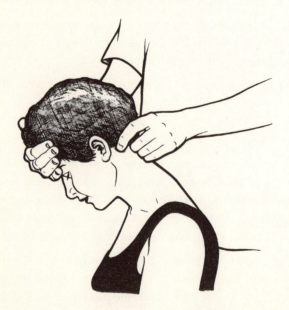

4. With your thumb and index finger, press firmly (as shown) on the bone at the base of the skull. Hold these points for about 15 seconds, and then stretch your hand to reach the bone behind the ears. Hold again, and then press your thumb into the "salt cellar" at the top of the spine where the head joins the neck. Massage

in a circular motion. Continue to support her forehead, and massage quite firmly at the base of the skull, using your thumb and fingers; make small, circular movements.

5. Now move onto the back of the neck, using your thumb and index finger on either side of her neck bones; hold for about 15 seconds, and then hold where the neck joins the shoulders. Then go over her neck again, using a circular movement.

6. Place your hands over her shoulders, with your fingers pointing toward her chest, and use your thumb or the heel of your hand to knead the muscles in a circular motion. I call this the "motion picture bit." You must have seen many screen idols having their shoulders massaged like this. Ask your partner if she would like you to go back to any sore place.

7. Put one arm across the top of your partner's chest and encourage her to relax forward onto it. With your other hand, continue massaging down one side of, but not on, the bones of the spine. Work in a similar fashion around the shoulder blade. Use your other arm, and repeat for the other side of the spine.

8. Stand in front of your partner, pick up her wrist, and shake her hand, letting it flop (unless there is pain in the joint). Ask her to imagine a heavy, wet sweater on a clothesline. You will feel her arm become heavier when she thinks heavy. Stretch her palm area, give her fingers a gentle pull, and then massage her hand. Next, hold her hand, and with your other hand, hook your thumb into the armpit on the same side as the hand. Give the arm a gentle pull. Repeat on the other side.

9. Stand behind your partner, support her head against your chest, and massage her temples in a circular fashion. Then stroke her brow with both index fingers, from the center outward. To release tension in the jaw, stroke or massage from her chin to behind each ear.

10. Finish off with a "magnetic" massage by stroking lightly and rapidly first down the head and then down the back and then down the arms and hands.

Sometimes people are quite sleepy after a head, neck, and shoulder massage. Your partner might need a short rest before helping you.

It is helpful for very tense people to have a daily massage. The therapeutic value of massage is becoming more widely recognized. Aromatherapy (massaging with the essential oil of plants), on the other hand, is only beginning to be an acceptable relaxation technique in the United States. However, many claim aromatherapy has a beneficial effect on the nervous system.

Further Exercises

QUICK TENSION RELEASE

This can be done almost anywhere: on a bus, on a plane, or at home. Sit down with your back straight, but not stiff; put your hands palm upward in your lap; and place your feet together, flat on the floor. Drop your head a little, and take a slow, complete breath. As you let your breath out, let your shoulders drop, and allow your thighs and knees to fall outward. Imagine a beautiful blue sparkling light that starts about a foot above your head; let it ripple through your body, out the soles of your feet, and down through the floor. Allow the light to take your tension with it. If you practice this exercise regularly, you will be surprised at how effective it is. You may also notice that it makes your feet tingle.

THE WET DOG SHAKE

Imagine that you are an old English sheepdog; you have been in the sea, and now you are shaking the water off your coat. Picture the dog: he shakes from head to tail. You do the same: hold onto something if you need to, and then change hands. Really let go and feel your cheeks wobble. If you have back problems, avoid this exercise.

LAUGHTER

Laughter is a great muscle relaxant. It also gives all your internal organs a massage.

Tight Muscles Pull Bones Out of Alignment

The skeletal system provides a movable framework that gives support and protection to the soft tissues. The spine, which consists of 33 irregular bones, serves as the main support for the trunk and neck, and gives protection to the spinal cord.

The Backbone

Ideally, the backbone is flexible and allows the trunk to move freely. Although each joint in the spine allows only slight movement, there are so many joints that they provide the potential for this flexibility. Many people, however, are afraid to move their spines, and suffer back pain and sciatica as a result.

The Backbone's Connected to . . .

Everything. The spinal nerves leave the spinal cord in pairs to service the whole body: the nerves in the neck and arms originate in the neck or cervical area; nerves in the abdomen and rib cage originate in the thoracic or chest area; the nerves in the lower back, hips, and legs originate in the lumbar area; and the nerves in the backs of the legs originate in the sacral area. This should give you some idea of the area of the spine your symptoms may be coming from: a pain in the knee, for example, might have nothing to do with the knee but may be coming from the spine.

How Can This Cause Panic Attacks?

Osteopaths and chiropractors believe that a straight, flexible spine means a healthy body, and that slight displacements of vertebrae, called subluxations, interfere with the nerve supply and can cause organic disease. Sometimes a subluxation will not cause pain in the spine, but will cause an internal organ to malfunction. The symptoms caused by spinal displacements correspond to the vertebrae concerned (for example, a displacement of the atlas, the first bone of the spine, can impede the flow of blood in the cerebral arteries and cause dizziness or a reduced glucose supply causing hypoglycemia—both causes of panic attacks). The most common cause of this particular displacement is repeatedly turning the head to one side to look at a badly placed television set or notes at the side of a computer. Lying on the stomach in bed and keeping the head in one position is another cause. Because circulation to the head is also affected by improper positions, dizziness can occur—and we have seen how becoming dizzy when you are outside is a potent trigger for a panic attack. If you have stiffness, or pain in the neck, and dizziness when you turn your head, see your doctor. If he or she cannot help you, consider having your neck adjusted by an osteopath or chiropractor. Your doctor may be able to recommend one.

Summary

There is no shortcut to unlocking muscles and finding emotional health. Many people have tried drugs for this purpose, but, this treatment often compounds the muscle spasms and emotional problems. It is scary to let go, and many times you will want to retreat to your prison, lock the gates, and remain there. Don't! Come out and try again. Don't be put off by people who feel threatened by the change in you. Your first duty is to yourself. There will be others who will welcome the new you.

CHAPTER TWELVE

Agoraphobia

Agoraphobia literally means "abnormal fear of crossing or of being in open or public places" (*Webster's Ninth New Collegiate Dictionary*), but the term is generally used to describe extreme fear of leaving the safety of the home. It can be a manifestation of severe anxiety or depression, or it can appear in a person who feels quite well until he tries to venture outdoors. Such people are often quite happy to go out if there is someone with them. Agoraphobia is an extremely distressing problem: the sufferer loses his freedom, self-reliance, and self-esteem, and also suffers physically because of insufficient sunshine, fresh air, and exercise.

Should I See the Doctor?

Your doctor will be able to tell you whether you are suffering from anxiety or depression, or both, and might feel you need help from drugs for a while, just to get you back into a more normal routine. (The dangers of long-term drug treatment have already been discussed.)

Your doctor might also refer you to a psychologist or therapist who can support you through counseling or desensitization therapy. This latter treatment is relaxation training plus gradual exposure to the situations you fear most, such as going into a store or traveling on a bus. You might be asked to make a list of everything you have to face that makes you afraid. Starting with the least fearsome, together you would gradually work through the list.

If your doctor cannot help you and you have already tried drugs, you have nothing to lose, and perhaps a great deal to gain, if you use the suggestions in this chapter. *Remember many people come through agoraphobia with nothing more than self-help.* Before you can progress, you need to accept the fact that although you might not even remember the incident, there is a memory tucked away in some corner of your mind that makes you react with fear in certain situations. If you are terribly anxious about everything, and going out just happens to be included, you probably need professional help. But that does not mean that you would not benefit from using self-help methods, too. In the same way that a tune or smell can bring back a memory you thought you had forgotten, the thought of being in a certain place or doing something, such as traveling in the subway, can dredge up a fear despite the fact that you might have no clear memory of when it originated.

What Plants These Rogue Thoughts in the Mind?

When agoraphobia is not part of a generally very anxious state, people can often remember the first time they had funny feelings outside. One man said he remembered having the identical feeling when he played in the street soon after he had measles. He was six years old at the time. Another man said he first had the "feeling" when he was 12: he was on a Sunday school outing and was hit by a bat. The feeling came again when, as an adult, he witnessed a car crash. It is often when a person is physically low that he has his first panic attack outside: after having the flu is very common.

When Thoughts Work in Your Favor

Imagine that you are sitting at home and you decide to play tennis or go out dancing. You start *thinking* about what you are going to do.

For example, My new tennis shoes are upstairs. I'll give Bill a ring. Or, Julie might be at the dance club. It was fun last time. This rehearsal releases the necessary chemicals in your brain for you to run for the ball, rock the night away, or whatever. Think of it: even before your bottom leaves the chair, this is happening; it's an exciting thought, because it helps to explain what happens in agoraphobia.

When Your Thoughts Work Against You

Again, imagine that you are sitting at home and you think with dread, I have to go to the supermarket. I hate going out. I might be sick. I might faint. What do you think the body is being flooded with in response to these thoughts? Yes, adrenaline. So the fear that these thoughts bring triggers overbreathing, and then your pulse races, you sweat, and all the dreaded feelings invade your mind. Think of it: this is before you even leave your chair—there is no real threat at all. In his article "Hyperventilation Syndromes in Medicine and Psychiatry," L. C. Lum, M.D., states that 60 percent of agoraphobes hyperventilate and 60 percent of hyperventilators are agoraphobic.

Following is my attempt at humor, which might help you see the lighter side of agoraphobia. (Agony Aunt is a tongue-in-cheek British term for "advice columnist.")

> Dear Agony Aunt—I'm an Agoraphobe
>
> It's panic that's driving me crazy
> I haven't been out for a week
> At the thought of crossing the threshold
> My breathing speeds up and I freak!

I know that agoraphobia is extremely distressing and frustrating, and that you can be as much a prisoner with this as you would be with two broken ankles, but think of it: changing your thinking would not get rid of the fractures, but *changing your thoughts can stop you from overbreathing, stop you from panicking, and cure your agoraphobia*. Let's stop using this term and talk about panicky feelings at the thought of going out, because that is *all* that agoraphobia is. Some people talk about "my agoraphobia" and feel affronted when I demystifiy it. They would rather think of it as an illness in itself, rather than a symptom of overstimulated nerves that will improve through effort. Fortunately, most people are delighted to have all anxiety symptoms explained and love the feeling that they can be in control of their panicky feelings.

How Can I Change My Thoughts?

I don't pretend that changing thoughts is easy, but it can be done. It involves understanding that the brain releases helpful chemicals when you give it the right thoughts, incorporating relaxation and visualization techniques into your life, and lots and lots of practice.

RELAXATION AND VISUALIZATION

Visualization involves making mental pictures to lead your body in the direction in which you want it to go. For example, if you are low in energy, during a relaxed state, when your body is ready to respond, you can visualize yourself as active and fit, absorbed in your favorite sport, and so on. If you want to quiet an overactive nervous system, you can imagine that you are drifting on a calm lake, that you are floating wrapped in a fluffy pink cloud, or that you are a baby being gently rocked in a crib. If you have a fever, you can imagine that a cool mountain stream is washing over you. If you have a pain, you can imagine that you are breathing soft pink light into the sore place with an "in" breath, and then sending the pain out through the soles of the feet and into the earth on the "out" breath. Don't dismiss these suggestions as half-baked: visualization can be very powerful. Choosing the right images is as personal as choosing the right diet: you know your fears, and you know what will make you feel safe.

PRACTICE THIS AT HOME

1. When you are not hungry and when you do not need to use the bathroom, find a warm, quiet place and either lie down or sit down.

2. Choose your image of a safe place. If you don't like any of the previous suggestions, what about lying on warm sand protected by a windbreak, listening to the sea. Or

what about sitting in a walled garden, listening to summer sounds. When you are where you want to be, practice gentle, complete breaths for ten minutes.

3. When you feel warm and relaxed, imagine yourself going into the situation you fear. Continuing to breathe slowly, repeat affirmative statements several times, statements such as, I am calm. This is easy. Mary, you are doing so well. I am doing better and better every day in every way. Repeat any words of comfort, praise, and reassurance you would like to hear, until the old fear is erased, and new, confident, calm thoughts gleam like jewels in your mind. If there are many situations that make you panic, start with the one that is the least fear provoking. As you conquer one, move on to the next.

4. Practice day after day. *Don't give up after two days and say this is not working—it takes* time.

You might think that this is not a very long chapter to cover such an enormous problem. Agoraphobia is a panic attack you experience outside, or at the thought of going outside. Other aspects of panic attacks have been covered in other chapters: breathing, unstable blood sugar levels, and tight muscles. If you are looking after these aspects of panic attacks, you should be more than halfway to curing your agoraphobia.

CHAPTER THIRTEEN

Worry and Panic

In headaches and worry life leaks away.

—W. H. Auden

Worry is a reaction to a problem to which you don't have an answer. In an attempt to find a solution, your brain works overtime and thought processes are speeded up. This almost goes without saying: it would be hard to imagine anyone worrying slowly!

It's easy to see why constant worriers are more likely to have panic attacks. It's only one small step from negative thoughts, such as, Life is always hard or I'm useless, to I can't cope or I'm going to faint, to a full-blown panic attack. We have talked a lot about the biological approach to panic: the effects of breathing, blood sugar, nutrition, supplements, and muscle tension. It is now time to discuss how you can promote yourself to managing director of your life: how you can retrain your fearful thoughts and order them to give up old habits and work with you instead of against you.

Worry: Productive and Unproductive

A degree of productive worry is good if it is used only for problem solving. For example, imagine that you are in the middle of a busy day at work when a glance at your calendar reminds you of a dinner party you had arranged for that evening. You barely know the couple but had enjoyed meeting them so much that you wanted to get better acquainted. Your mind starts to spin when you realize that the house is a mess, there's only a tub of margarine and half of last night's pizza in the refrigerator, there's a lot of ice cubes but nothing else in the freezer, your only decent dress is at the cleaners, and your hair needs washing. Do you get the feeling? Because you are worried, the problem solving starts: The house is a mess! I could call Lucy and ask her to do a quick tidying up for me. Oh dear, the meal, I'll never fix it in time. I could go to the deli at lunchtime. No home cooking, I can't do that. No one will know it's store-bought if I add sour cream and a few chives to the soup. If I call them now and ask them if they can make it 8 p.m. instead of 7:30, I can collect my dress on the way home, and if I wash my hair as soon as I get in, it should be fine by 8. Worry, worry, worry, all done, problem solved.

The opposite of this is unproductive worry. This can start out as looking for a solution and then the worry gets out of hand. What if there is no solution to the problem, or there is no action that can be taken, and yet the worry goes on and on, around and around, like a hamster on a wheel? This is the type of worry we need to get rid of. The trouble is, the thought process is often so ingrained that we become almost addicted to it: it is what we know, and at the slightest anxiety, or even without an apparent trigger, we worry, worry, worry. The thoughts of the continual worrier are often as follows:

—What if she dies before I do?

—What if I miss that train?

—What if the dog gets run over?

—What if my refusal hurts her feelings?

—What if I fail?

—What if I have a panic attack?

—What if something awful happens?

—What if there's an earthquake?

—What if I wear that suit and it gets a spot on it?

Worrying like this is called anticipatory anxiety. This type of anxiety is understandable if you are afraid of the dentist and your appointment is soon, but the majority of these worried thoughts are fearful, negative thoughts that result from having an exhausted nervous system. It would be impossible for someone whose nervous system was in a healthy state to spend the day worrying about a succession of events that were extremely unlikely to occur. Healthy people are relaxed and just get on with life, possibly thinking about how pleasurable or productive they can make their day.

The Way Forward

You are probably only too aware that entreaties to stop worrying—"For heaven's sake, stop worrying! You worry about every little thing!"—make you feel a great deal worse, because they add guilt and blame to your unhappy state. You would change it if you only knew how. It's like asking someone not to cough when she has bronchitis!

Fighting your feelings causes you to tense up your muscles, speed up your breathing, and so on—all the damaging triggers that by now you know so well. These feelings will not kill you, they will not make you ill. Allow them to happen and repeat something like, "It will pass, it will pass." Only when you give up fighting will the feelings lessen in intensity, and only then will you finally be in control. Claire Weekes, author of a self-help book on nerves, stresses the need to go along with the feelings and not fight them. Her formula is as follows:

Accepting/Floating/Letting Time Pass

Accepting

The first step is to accept that excessive worry is a symptom, not an inevitable part of being you. When your nerves recover, you will worry less. If you have no counselor or person who can keep gently reminding you of this, then write notes to yourself and put them on the refrigerator door, by the telephone, and on your bedside table. Acceptance is vital: you cannot take the next step without fully believing that worrying about the worrying, and continually looking inward for solutions—going over and over the symptoms—will just compound your problem. Fear $\rightarrow$ adrenaline $\rightarrow$ more fear. Relaxation $\rightarrow$ peace $\rightarrow$ more relaxation. In a panic attack you have experienced the worst of the anxiety symptoms: there is a limit to how many awful feelings there are, although you might find it hard to believe that. But how could acceptance of worrying or panic make things any worse? Think about what you have read about how your body reacts to your mood.

Floating

Some people say, "But how do you 'float'?" It is really what it says, floating along with the feelings, moving with them and coming out the other side. You will see that far from losing control, you gain control: I'm not afraid of you; you are only feelings. You will vanish when I learn to relax more and stop worrying. This takes practice and courage. And remember, you are the only one who can slow your breathing; you are the only one who can let your tight muscles relax. Choose an image to help you float: perhaps see yourself in a boat floating down a gently flowing river, or safe in a fluffy pink cloud, or holding the hand of a trusted friend. Visualize yourself in your floating scene several times a day, and link it to a short command: for example, "Boat." This in time will replace the panicky thoughts: I can't cope, I'll be sick, and so on. The negative images and thoughts need to be firmly and repeatedly replaced by comforting thoughts and relaxing images.

Worrying is like any other nervous habit: just as people who are nail biters keep straying unconsciously to their mouths, so the worrying thoughts come uninvited into the mind and start their endless chatter. When you "wake up" (bring them into your conscious mind) and discuss these thoughts with yourself, you can order them to "Stop" or "Go away."

Letting Time Pass

Allowing time to pass is very difficult for the nervous person. Yes, you are desperate to get rid of these awful feelings, but unfortunately it takes time: you will have to be patient. You will also have to accept that there will be times when you think it's not going to work and you feel as discouraged as ever. Nature does not heal in a straight line: it's normal to go up and down. Keep in mind the physiological fact that nervous tissue (the cells from which the nerves are made) takes longer to heal than skin, muscles, or bones. This might help you to keep things in perspective.

Can Family and Friends Help?

Ask family and friends to gently remind you to relax when the worrying thoughts start to spill out. You might feel slightly irritated or hurt when they do this, but it will serve to help your awareness of the problem. And it will also prevent what commonly happens in this situation, namely that the sufferer goes on and on, while onlookers keep quiet until they can stand it no longer and then explode. This is disastrous for all concerned. A gentler approach is for family and friends to remind the sufferer that talking about the symptoms all the time just reinforces them.

Family and friends should bear in mind that in continually talking about the symptoms, the sufferer is looking for a way out, an answer, and he might think you unfeeling if you take this approach. The sufferer will benefit more by having constant reassurance withheld until a time that feelings can be discussed. Keep to that time, although waiting might produce anger or tears. The important message for the sufferer is, The answer is within you. The most positive thing family and friends can do is to read this book and work with the sufferer: do the exercises and listen to relaxation tapes together.

CHAPTER FOURTEEN

Exercise, Daylight, Sunlight, and Fresh Air

Exercise

When people realize that they are inviting the disease process to take over if they don't exercise, they become much more committed to following a program. When you slow down your circulation by inactivity, organic functions become sluggish. For example, when the digestive system slows down, you become constipated. Muscles are also affected by inactivity: they lack nourishment and build up crystals, which are formed from the waste products of digestion. The rubbish disposal system of the body, the lymphatic system, cannot work properly if the body is inactive.

Why Does the Lymphatic System Need Movement?

The lymphatic system is part of the body's defense against disease. A clear, watery body fluid called lymph, which relies on muscle contraction for its circulation, is carried through a complex network of small vessels that carry cellular refuse on the way. This refuse is then passed into the bloodstream, where it is processed. Unlike the circulatory system, the lymphatic system has no pump: if you don't move, the lymph slows down. This can result in a collection of fluid in the tissues, and a depressed immune system. In addition, some cells in the body that rely on lymph for their nourishment become malnourished. Even if you have to stay in bed for some reason, you can still help to circulate the lymph by gently squeezing each group of muscles in turn, and rotating the ankles and wrists. Massage can also be very helpful.

START SLOWLY

Take care not to rush into frenetic activity if you have been sitting around for months. A few conditions—for instance, chronic fatigue syndrome (myalgic encephalomyelitis)—do not respond to exercise. That said, however, most problems do respond to gentle exercise. Check with your doctor if you are unsure. Build up the amount of exercise you do slowly. Some people are so out of touch with their bodies that they are very resistant to the idea of exercise.

Gentle Seated Movements with Visualization

If you have been inactive, perhaps you should start with seated exercises. As you do this routine, visualize anything that suggests improved circulation: slow streams becoming fast-flowing rivers, pipes being unblocked, or anything else that comes to mind. Bring life to your circulation!

EXERCISE

1. Place your feet in front of you, about a foot apart. Drop your shoulders and look at the floor a few feet in front of you. This will stop you from shortening the muscles at the sides of the neck; these shortened muscles are part of the "iron collar" of tension.

2. Take one complete breath. Breathing in through the nose, imagine your breath rising up through your feet.

Let the breath expand your abdomen, and then your ribs, and then take the breath up into the shoulders. Open your mouth as you let the breath out, and imagine that you are filled with a bright color of your choice.

3. Breathe normally, while you lift the shoulders toward the ears and then let the shoulders drop toward the floor. Repeat eight times, if you can.

4. Keeping the corresponding arm limp, circle each shoulder in a clockwise direction eight times. Then try doing the shoulders together.

5. To stretch the neck, allow your head to fall to the right, bring it back to the center, and then allow it to drop to the left; repeat four times on each side. Don't raise your shoulders to meet your ears.

6. Stretch both arms to the ceiling, and then let them fall loosely toward the floor.

7. Stretch out your fingers, and then draw eight circles, in each direction, with your forefingers.

8. To exercise your legs, draw the same circles with each big toe in turn.

9. For the buttocks and thighs, tighten these muscles and feel yourself rise in your seat.

10. Finish this session by shaking all over like a wet dog.

Fear of shaking in public is often a reason why a person stays indoors. Regularly doing the wet dog exercise is very helpful. It takes a lot more energy to hold shaking in than to let it out. Have a good shake whenever you feel tense and particularly before any social event that worries you. If you feel panicky while you are out, find a restroom, let your jaw go loose, and allow yourself to shake from your head down to your toes.

If you are resistant to setting aside a special time to exercise, start building exercise into your daily life: a few stretches, shakes, or wrist and foot movements at your desk, when watching television, at the kitchen sink, or while you are on the telephone. These exercises are useful if you do not feel up to swimming, walking, or more strenuous exercise. Remember what happens to your circulation if you don't move!

Perhaps the next stage of exercise could be walking briskly for 30 minutes a day, and then progressing to aerobic exercise. It is easier and safer to have some supervision for aerobic exercise. Join a class or take the advice of a fitness trainer at a gym. Exercising might feel like a terrible chore at first, but keep going: once you feel the benefits, you will become more enthusiastic.

Daylight

Biologists have discovered that light is not only essential to health, but that requirements for light vary as much from person to person as do requirements for vitamins. Daylight is necessary for the normal functioning of the brain as well as for the regulation of the wake-sleep cycle. Therefore, your nervous problems are compounded if you are housebound with agoraphobia. Even if you are severely agoraphobic, you can sit at an open window, without your glasses, for at least 20 minutes during the brightest part of the day. Also, avoid turning day into night. This gives you a feeling of having permanent jet lag and leads to further depression. It's hard to get out of bed in the morning if you are depressed, but it is the only way to progress.

Sunlight

Sunlight lifts the spirit, makes vitamins, kills germs, and revitalizes us. It is foolish to lie and bake in the sun for long periods, but unless you have a sun allergy it is unwise to *continually* walk around covered in sun block, wearing dark glasses. *Brief* exposure to sun and air is necessary for the health of the skin and the production of vitamin D. You risk depression if you never allow daylight to enter the eye and stimulate the pineal gland.

Fresh Air

Much has been said in this book about breathing. When you are taking your wonderful, complete breaths, don't do it where the air is stale. Air contaminated by smoke or fumes is easy to recognize, but there are other causes of stale air that are not as well known.

POSITIVE IONS

Air contains positively and negatively charged particles. We breathe in these particles and absorb them through our skin (interestingly enough, at our acupuncture points). An excess of positively charged particles, which occurs before a storm, during spells of hot wind, and in "sick" buildings—where computers and other electrical equipment are located in poorly ventilated areas—causes respiratory problems, headaches, irritability, digestive problems, anxiety, and depression. The effect on the nervous system is powerful, making positive ions a potential trigger for panic attacks.

When there are positive ions, the brain overproduces a chemical called serotonin, which, in turn, can produce nasal congestion, lethargy, and a feeling of being sticky (not the same feeling as being too hot) and swollen.

The oppressive feeling before an electrical storm best describes this phenomenon: restlessness, feeling "under the weather." We can also experience the effects of positive ions in cities where stale air is trapped between tall buildings, or when we sit in stuffy rooms surrounded by plastic and electrical equipment, wearing clothes made from synthetic fibers.

NEGATIVE IONS

Negative ions, on the other hand, have a tonic effect on the nervous system and reduce histamine levels in the blood. As any allergy sufferer knows, histamine is strongly associated with unpleasant feelings. The benefits of negative ions are becoming widely known, not only for cleaning the air, killing bacteria and viruses, but also as a treatment for asthma, bronchitis, migraine headaches, burns, scalds, and wounds.

Those with irritable bowel syndrome can also benefit from negatively charged air. An interesting book on this subject, *The Ion Effect* by Fred Soyka (Bantam, 1978), describes the effect of positive ions on the mind and body.

WEATHER-SENSITIVE PEOPLE

After a thunderstorm, the air is negatively charged: it smells fresh and you experience "the calm *after* the storm." Your energy returns and your mood improves. The air by the sea, waterfalls, and flowing water—even a shower—is also negatively charged and can produce a feeling of well-being. Some people are more affected by this than others, in the same way that some people are irritable and restless when there is a full moon, and others do not notice it. (During a full moon, the positively charged layer of the ionosphere is pushed nearer to the Earth, increasing the number of positive ions in the air we breathe.)

AVOID BEING BOMBARDED WITH POSITIVE IONS

To keep your exposure to positive ions to a minimum, make sure your home is well ventilated, and avoid nylon sheets, carpets, and clothes, if possible. At work, take frequent breaks from computer screens. Consider buying an ionizer (a small machine that negatively charges the air) and a screen protector for your computer. Ionizers are available in most large hardware stores; you may have to look in an alternative health magazine for an address for a computer screen protector. If you drive a lot, you could fit a small ionizer in the car. This greatly reduces the effects of pollution as well as preventing car sickness. Many drivers have reported that they feel less tired at the end of the day.

You cannot overuse negative ions. There is no maximum dosage: you can breathe in as many as you like. Some people have ionizers in every room. If you have one in your family room, don't forget to put it by your bed at night: it will help you to have a restful night.

WHAT ELSE CAN I DO TO ERADICATE POSITIVE IONS?

Walking by the sea and taking a shower were mentioned earlier as ways to escape positive ions. You can also try magnetic massage. This simply means stroking with the fingertips, using a feather-light touch, from the top of the head down the arms, chest, and abdomen as far as you can reach, and then flicking your hands after a few strokes to throw off the positive ions. If you don't flick your hands, they will become heavy and sticky. Do this for anyone who is rest-less or has a headache. There is a limit to how much of your body you can reach when you are doing it for yourself, but when doing it for someone else, it is useful to stroke from the head to the base of the spine; then take your hands to the side, and shake away what you have collected. Do this for about five minutes and then wash your hands. Invariably, the recipient will say that she feels lighter after this massage.

(If after using this technique, you become interested in using your hands, you might want to read Dolores Kreiger's *Therapeutic Touch: How to Use Your Hands to Help or Heal*. It is rather wordy, but don't be put off by that, because it does give information about using the human energy field for healing. This is a fascinating subject. Dolores Kreiger is a nurse who first researched this subject in the 1970s and gave it the name therapeutic touch.)

Therapeutic Touch

Your heart, brain, muscles, and nerves all run on a delicate form of electricity. Although you do not need to be plugged into a wall socket to operate, you are still an electrical being, surrounded by an electro-magnetic field. In the 1930s, two Russian scientists, Semyon and Valentina Kirlian, experimented with photography that clearly showed this field. One of the first people to study what he called the L-fields, or the life fields, and how they affect health, was Harold Saxon Burr, M.D., of Yale University Medical School, who began his work in the 1950s. Robert O. Becker, a leading researcher on electro-magnetic pollution, believes that electromagnetic fields around power lines and electrical appliances can cause depression, a sup-pressed immune system, and other health problems. The research of Burr, Becker, and others suggests that disturbances in your electrical field develop before illness in your physical body does. This could be the medicine of the future: the prevention and treatment of illness through correcting faults in our electromagnetic fields. This knowl-edge is not new. Similar methods can be found in ancient forms of healing.

CAN I FEEL MY OWN ELECTRICAL FIELD?

Only 1 percent of the population can't feel their electrical field, so try it. You might have to try on a few occasions before you can be sure, but the more you practice, the more sensitive your hands will become. The movements you use to build up the field between your hands is like the movements you would make when playing an accordion slowly.

EXERCISE

1. Sit in an upright chair, with your back straight but not tense. Drop your shoulders and breathe slowly from the abdomen. It's best if you can continue to breathe this way while you are following the rest of the exercise, but if you can't, just do a few slow breaths before you start.

2. Stretch your fingers out wide, and become aware of the palms of your hands.

3. Rub your hands together briskly for about 15 seconds.

4. Hold the hands about eight inches apart, and then gradually bring them toward each other until they are about one inch apart, but do not let them touch.

5. Separate the hands again, this time to about six inches apart, and then bring them toward each other, again without touching.

6. This time, bring them together and bounce them together: remember to keep the hands relaxed. You will feel a resistance, or a feeling of pressure, between your hands. Some people say that they feel as if there is foam rubber between their hands; others describe feelings of heat, tingling, throbbing, or pulling.

Using Therapeutic Touch on Yourself

Therapeutic touch is much like magnetic massage, using the same flowing movements, but this time you don't touch your body. Now that your hands are energized, you can use them to clear congestion, increase relaxation, and ease discomfort. Take a few complete breaths and consciously think about caring for yourself.

EXERCISE

1. Take a footbath that includes five drops of lavender or marjoram essential oil, or simply massage under the arches of your feet for about one minute. If your feet are very tense, take a little more time on them. Then place them flat on the floor if you will sit throughout this exercise.

2. Sit relaxed, or lie on the floor or bed. Slow down your breathing.

3. Close your eyes and imagine yourself totally well and peaceful. If this image escapes you, use the mental affirmation, I am totally well and peaceful. Imagine that a pure white light is entering your head, filling your body, and radiating out of your fingers and palms. Reach up beyond your head and stroke, about three to four inches above your body, just as though you were touching something solid; continue down over your face, neck, chest, and abdomen; and then sweep your hands to either side of your body and flick your hands to throw off the positive ions. This last step is important because you need to remove the congestion from your body. You will feel prickling or heat in your hands as you pick up positive ions. You can just flick them off, as though you were shaking water from your hands, in the same way you did with the magnetic massage.

4. Continue stroking for about ten minutes or until your arms feel tired.

5. Still imagining that you are filled with white light, place the hands on the tops of the thighs, where they join the body, and if you can cross the left foot over the right foot comfortably, do so. If not, then just have

your feet touching, with the hands on the tops of the thighs. Stay there for as long as you feel you want to.

Currently, there is a great deal of research going on with regard to therapeutic touch. It is a gentle, inexpensive treatment, free from drugs, that not only has a profound effect on the nervous system, but is also "soul therapy" for many people. If you deny that you have a soul, or spirit, and believe that you have only a body and a personality, then the next chapter is not for you.

CHAPTER FIFTEEN

Loving the Inner Child

The truth about our childhood is stored up in our body and although we can repress it, we can never alter it. Our intellect can be deceived, our feelings manipulated. . . . But someday the body will present its bill, for it is as incorruptible as a child who, still whole in spirit, will accept no compromise or excuses, and it will not stop tormenting us until we stop evading the truth.

—Margaret Atwood, *True Stories*

Who Are You?

We have seen that when you let go of the protection of rigid muscles and shallow breathing, you can feel enormous emotional release, bringing you much nearer to finding out who you really are. Another way you can get nearer to your real being is to make a conscious, loving decision to get to know the spirit of the child in you, who may well have been "squashed" during your growing years; to connect again with the spontaneity and joy that is the birthright of every human being.

Growth is not possible without pain. It is scary and difficult to leave behind outgrown thoughts that have kept you cemented behind your wall of neuroses. Part of your fear is that if you open up and go down to your soul level, you don't know how much is going to be there. It's like opening Pandora's box: you may wonder, What will be there? Will it overwhelm me? Will I feel worse than I do now? Will it kill me? All these questions make you want to keep your protective guard up, to settle down again behind the wall, *but look at what the cost could be*: physical illness, chronic anxiety, depression, or even disintegration of your personality.

You could choose to half-live. But if you want to be whole, something has to give. I don't pretend that it is easy to clear away years of accumulated "soul garbage," the garbage you have kept there by all your addictions, not just to drink, drugs, or food, but also to work, relationships, perfection, exercise, or compulsive talking. Your lack of inner vision also keeps you firmly stuck where you are.

How Can I Make Contact with the Child Within?

A helpful book on developing a relationship with the child within is *Healing Your Aloneness: Finding Love and Wholeness Through Your Inner Child* by Erica J. Chopich and Margaret Paul (Harper & Row, 1990). This book can help you to build a nurturing balance between the adult in you and your inner child. It describes a self-healing process that can be used every day to get rid of self-destructive patterns and fears. Another valuable resource is Louise Hay's book *You Can Heal Your Life.* (Eden Grove Editions, 1984). She believes that you are 100 percent responsible for all your experiences and that every thought you think creates your future. She says you have the power to change things in the present only, not the past, and that when you really love yourself, everything in your life works. She also stresses that you must release the past and forgive everyone. Some people are able to bring together the adult part and the child part of the personality through drama, dance, painting, or writing. Artistic expression gives your inner child a voice.

My own inner child rebelled, grabbed me by the throat, and poured out a stream of complaints in writing a few years ago. The complaints came in the form of poetry, which mystified me, because I knew nothing about writing in this form and had never taken any interest in poetry. In fact, until several years ago, the only writing I had done of any kind since nursing days was a shopping list or an entreaty to some teacher to save one of my offspring from some hated physical activity! Nowadays, however, my inner child is my muse.

Wouldn't It Be Easy

If we could just call Mr. Dyno-rod

When expression freezes

And moribund feelings choke our life canal;

A banal thought, perhaps,

But if he could poke and prod

And suddenly, if without fears or tears,

All that greasy-grime of grueling years

Could go with a glorious glug down the plug,

Wouldn't it be nice.

It would also be nice

Not to have to pay the price

To be a pilgrim.

I believe that through the inner child you not only have access to who you really are, but that the inner child is your direct communication with your God-spark: your soul, spirit, psyche. And if you have not integrated your inner child into your personality, how can you reach further and connect with your Creator, God, Allah, the Great Spirit, Universal Energy, Unconditional Love: the Love that passes all understanding? If you are cut off from yourself, how can you love God? How can you love your fellow human beings? Jung calls the process of bringing the soul and the personality together individuation. It can be a battle.

How can I nurture this child

Sickly, yet wild with a strength

Which has me beaten; I know she's just,

But I'm weary of her uprightness, her persistence.

Be Yourself, Not What Others Think You Should Be

Laughter is a great defense against panic. It provides an internal massage and releases tension. Here is a little story I have written about Terence, who loved himself just as he was. I hope it makes you smile. (*Mashed swede*, to a Briton, means "mashed rutabaga.")

Terence the Tiger

I'm Terence the tiger
A tiger gone wrong.
I'm not bold, I'm not fierce, I'm not snarling
I'm kind and polite, a furry delight,
And always everyone's darling.
I love bunny rabbits, and chipmunks, and frogs,
And cute little kittens, and bold little dogs.
Folks can laugh, they can jeer, they can tease or deride,
I am what I am, marshmallow inside.
They can point, they can wink, or shout namby-pamby,
I refuse to eat deer; could you eat a Bambi?
I'll feed on mashed swede and the love that abounds
And have Tigger to tea when my birthday comes round.

May the love and light
of the Creator shine
on you as you journey
Toward self and the Infinite.

(Poems from an unpublished collection, *Finding the Thou in You*.)

Index

Meals, rushed, 40–41

Medications. *See* Drugs, prescribed

Memory, 28

Migraine headaches, 47, 49

Mineral supplements, 54, 62,
80–81

Morbid thoughts, 5, 20

Mouth breathing, 70

Muscles
aches, 47–48
spasms, 18–19, 29, 83–96
tension, 24

Neck tension, 18, 91–94

Negative ions, 64, 111–13

Nerves, exhausted, 16–21
and chronic muscle spasms,
18–19
emotional signs, 19–20
physical signs, 17–18

Niacin, 62

Niacinamide, 62, 80

Nicotine, 57, 60–62

Nose breathing, 70

Nose problems, 9, 28

Numbness, 29

Obesity, 49

Overbreathing. *See*
Hyperventilation

Oxazepam, 56

Pain, 9

Palpitations, 5, 17, 28, 42

Pancreas, 39, 45

Panic attacks
and agoraphobia, 7–8, 97–101
and blood sugar, 8, 17–18,
38–50, 77–82
and breathing, 22–37, 75–76
causes, 8–10, 16–21
and chronic muscle spasms,
83–96
definition, 3
and exhausted nerves, 16–21
experience of, 4
medical treatment, 11–15
symptoms, 5–6
types, 6–8
and worry, 102–106

Paradoxical reaction, 55

Paranoia, 20

Perception, heightened, 5

Phobias, 20, 28

Positive ions, 64, 111–13, 115

Prana, 68–69

Pranayama, 23

Premenstrual syndrome, 48,
80–81

Prescribed drugs. *See* Drugs, prescribed

Protein, 54, 78, 82

Provocation test, 25–26, 29

Prozac, 57

Quick tension release exercise, 94

Rapid speech, 19

Rapid thoughts, 20

Ulysses Press Health Books

A Natural Approach Books

Written in a friendly, nontechnical style, *A Natural Approach* books address specific health issues and show you how to take an active part in your own treatment. Whether you suffer from panic attacks, endometriosis or depression, each book will provide you with a thorough understanding of your condition and detail organic solutions that offer immediate relief for your symptoms and effectively remedy their underlying causes.

Believing that disease is more than a combination of symptoms, these books offer integrated mind/body programs that take a positive, preventative approach. Since traditional drug therapy is not always the best solution (and can sometimes be the problem), these guides show how to use alternative treatments to supplement or replace conventional medicine.

ANXIETY & DEPRESSION
ISBN 1-56975-118-8, 144 pp, $9.95

CANDIDA
ISBN 1-56975-153-6, 208 pp, $11.95

ENDOMETRIOSIS
ISBN 1-56975-088-2, 184 pp, $9.95

FREE YOURSELF FROM TRANQUILIZERS & SLEEPING PILLS
ISBN 1-56975-074-2, 192 pp, $9.95

IRRITABLE BLADDER & INCONTINENCE
ISBN 1-56975-089-0, 112 pp, $8.95

IRRITABLE BOWEL SYNDROME
2nd edition, ISBN 1-56975-188-9, 256 pp, $13.95

MIGRAINES
ISBN 1-56975-140-4, 240 pp, $10.95

PANIC ATTACKS
2nd edition, ISBN 1-56975-187-0, 144 pp, $9.95

The Natural Remedy Books

As home remedies and alternative treatments become increasingly accepted into the medical mainstream, people want information—not just hype and unproven claims—about the remedies they see in health food stores. *The Natural Remedy* books detail how these natural remedies have been used throughout history and how to safely incorporate them into an overall plan for maintaining good health.

CIDER VINEGAR
ISBN 1-56975-141-2, 144 pp, $8.95

GARLIC
ISBN 1-56975-097-1, 152 pp, $9.95

Discover Handbooks

Easy to follow and authoritative, *Discover* handbooks reveal an array of alternative therapies from around the world and demonstrate how to incorporate them into a program of good health.

Each book opens with information on the history and principles of the particular technique, then presents practical and straightforward guidance on ways in which it can be applied. Offering the tools needed to achieve and maintain an optimal state of health, the approach is one of personal improvement and self-reliance. Each of the books features: an introduction to the discipline; an explanation of its philosophy; step-by-step guide to its implementation; clear diagrams and charts; and case studies.

DISCOVER AYURVEDA
ISBN 1-56975-081-5, 128 pp, $8.95

DISCOVER COLOR THERAPY
ISBN 1-56975-093-9, 144 pp, $8.95

DISCOVER ESSENTIAL OILS
ISBN 1-56975-080-7, 128 pp, $8.95

DISCOVER MEDITATION
ISBN 1-56975-113-7, 144 pp, $8.95

DISCOVER NUTRITIONAL THERAPY
ISBN 1-56975-135-8, 120 pp, $8.95

DISCOVER OSTEOPATHY
ISBN 1-56975-115-3, 132 pp, $8.95

DISCOVER REFLEXOLOGY
ISBN 1-56975-112-9, 132 pp, $8.95

DISCOVER SHIATSU
ISBN 1-56975-082-3, 128 pp, $8.95

The Ancient and Healing Arts Books

The Ancient and Healing Arts books recount the development of healing art forms that have been used for thousands of years. Beautifully illustrated with full color on every page, they discuss the benefits of these time-honored techniques and offer detailed instructions on their use.

THE ANCIENT AND HEALING ART OF
AROMATHERAPY
ISBN 1-56975-094-7, 96 pp, $14.95

THE ANCIENT AND HEALING ART OF
CHINESE HERBALISM
ISBN 1-56975-139-0, 96 pp, $14.95

Other Health Titles

THE BOOK OF KOMBUCHA
ISBN 1-56975-049-1, 160 pp, $11.95
Explains the benefits of and addresses concerns about Kombucha, the widely used Chinese "tea mushroom."

HEALING REIKI: REUNITE MIND, BODY AND SPIRIT WITH HEALING ENERGY
ISBN 1-56975-162-5, 128 pp, $16.95
Examines the meaning, attitudes and history of Reiki while providing practical tips for receiving and giving this universal life energy.

HEPATITIS C: A PERSONAL GUIDE TO GOOD HEALTH
2nd edition, ISBN 1-56975-183-8, 180 pp, $13.95
Identifies the causes and symptoms of hepatitis C and presents conventional and alternative treatments for coping with the disease.

KNOW YOUR BODY: THE ATLAS OF ANATOMY
2nd edition, ISBN 1-56975-166-8, 160 pp, $12.95
Provides a a comprehensive, full-color guide to the human body.

MOOD FOODS
ISBN 1-56975-023-8, 192 pp, $11.95
Shows how the foods you eat influence your emotions and behavior.

NEW AGAIN!: THE 28-DAY DETOX PLAN FOR BODY AND SOUL
ISBN 1-56975-190-0, 128 pp, $16.95
Allows you to free your body *and* mind from toxins and live a healthy and balanced life.

THE 7 HEALING CHAKRAS: UNLOCKING YOUR BODY'S ENERGY CENTERS
ISBN 1-56975-168-4, 240 pp, $14.95
Explores the essence of chakras, vortices of energy that connect the physical body with the spiritual.

SEX HERBS: NATURE'S SEXUAL ENHANCERS
ISBN 1-56975-185-4, 140 pp, $12.95
Presents detailed descriptions of safe, natural products that boost sexual desire and pleasure.

YOUR NATURAL PREGNANCY: A GUIDE TO COMPLEMENTARY THERAPIES
ISBN 1-56975-059-9, 240 pp, $16.95
Details alternative therapies ranging from aromatherapy to yoga that can benefit pregnant women.

———————————

To order these books call 800-377-2542 or 510-601-8301, fax 510-601-8307, e-mail ulysses@ulyssespress.com, or write to Ulysses Press, P.O. Box 3440, Berkeley, CA 94703-3440. All retail orders are shipped free of charge. California residents must include sales tax. Allow two to three weeks for delivery.

About the Author

Shirley Trickett trained as a nurse before becoming a counselor and teacher. She is based in the northeast of England and travels both throughout the United Kingdom and abroad with her work. She has worked with anxious and depressed people for several years, and is the author of *Anxiety & Depression: A Natural Approach* (Ulysses Press, 1997), *Candida: A Natural Approach* (Ulysses Press, 1999), *Free Yourself from Tranquilizers and Sleeping Pills* (Ulysses Press, 1997), *Recipes for Health: Candida Albicans Yeast-Free and Sugar-Free Recipes* (Thorsons, 1994), and *The Irritable Bowel Syndrome and Diverticulosis* (Thorsons, 1990). She is the recipient of the Whitbread Community Care Award for her work with people withdrawing from tranquilizers and sleeping pills.